1964

WHAT A YEAR TO BE BORN!

Written by
Robin Bennett-Freebairn and Joe Toussaint

Published by Emersive
www.whatayeartobeborn.com

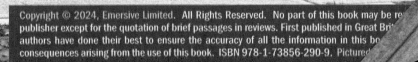

What happened in 1964? Most of us have a special affinity for the year we were born, but how much do we really know about it? This guide takes you through the highs and lows of an historic year at the end of the baby boom generation. The colour-coded chapters unlock a wealth of information, bringing you closer to what life was like in this special year.

Contents

▶ Introduction

On New Year's Day, Britain woke up to slightly below seasonal temperatures. However there was to be no repeat of the bitterly cold winter of 1963. Instead, it was the southern states of America who suffered unseasonable weather. Meridian in Mississippi saw a record 15 inches of snow. Those born in 1964 were the very last to be part of the post-war population bulge which defined those born between 1946 and 1964, known as 'Baby Boomers'. The most popular girls' names of the year were Susan, Julie and Karen, for boys it was David, Paul and Andrew. Beatlemania, which had already taken hold in Britain, now swept over the States. As part of the Fab Four's only world tour, they played to packed houses across North America. In April, they occupied the entire top five in the Billboard chart. Women were keen to sport a bikini on the beach and, courtesy of designer Mary Quant's mini-skirt, British women were beginning to wear skirts well above the knee. Many men embraced 'Mod' fashion, sporting three piece suits, cravats and crisp-pointed collared shirts. This pitted them against another sub-culture, the Rockers. Dressed in black leather, with greased back hair and riding motorbikes, the Rockers immersed themselves in early rock'n'roll. When the two cultures met there was often violence, particularly at seaside resorts.

There was also great political change in Britain. It was out with the old and in with the new, as pipe-smoking Harold Wilson led the Labour Party to victory, ending thirteen years of Conservative rule. In the world of media, things were changing quickly. On January 1st *Top of the Pops* first aired on the BBC channel, which had to change its name to BBC1, with the advent of BBC2 later in the year. Youngsters were kept in suspense when *Playschool* came to our screens in April. Would it be the round, arched or square window? Despite the efforts of the BBC, their output still seemed fairly staid. However, the birth of pirate radio, in the form of Radio Caroline arrived to give the youth the edginess they craved.

In world politics, Nelson Mandela and co-defendants were sentenced to life imprisonment in Apartheid South Africa. Meanwhile another civil rights activist, Martin Luther King Jr. was awarded the Nobel Peace Prize. In science, Dorothy Hodgkin was awarded the Nobel Prize in Chemistry, only to be greeted with tabloid headlines such as "British Wife Wins Nobel Prize".

In sport, the Olympic Games were held in Tokyo and the Olympic flame was brought into the stadium by a man born on the same day that the atomic bomb was dropped on Hiroshima. In boxing, Cassius Clay defeated Sonny Liston against all the odds. Shortly afterwards he joined the Nation of Islam and changed his name to Muhammed Ali. In film, the two highest grossing movies were both musicals, namely *Mary Poppins* and *My Fair Lady*. The literary world was sad to see the loss of Bond author Ian Fleming and the poet and socialite Edith Sitwell.

The Daily Headlines

No: 5706

Price: Three pence

Evening Edition

Friday, March 27, 1964

THE EARTHQUAKE THAT SHOOK ALASKA IS THE SECOND MOST POWERFUL EVER RECORDED

The Daily Headlines

Price: Three pence

Saturday, April 4, 1964

No: 5714

Evening Edition

THE BEATLES STORM AMERICA BY TAKING ALL TOP 5 SPOTS IN THE US BILLBOARD TOP 100 CHART

The Daily Headlines

Price: Three pence

Friday, July 17, 1964

No: 5812

Evening Edition

DONALD CAMPBELL SETS NEW WORLD LAND SPEED RECORD IN HIS BLUEBIRD CN7 AT 403.10MPH

The Daily Headlines

No: 5909

Evening Edition

Price: Three pence

Thursday, October 15, 1964

HAROLD WILSON BECOMES NEW PRIME MINISTER AFTER LABOUR NARROWLY BEATS THE CONSERVATIVES IN THE GENERAL ELECTION

Jan 1st It is Happy New Year all round for lovers of pop music as *Top of the Pops* first appears on our screens. Dusty Springfield's *I only Want Be with You* is the first song performed. The first band to appear are the Rolling Stones singing *I Wanna Be Your Man*.

Jan 1st Idlewild Airport in New York is renamed John F. Kennedy Airport. Baggage tags labelled IDL will now read JFK.

Jan 4th Pope Paul VI becomes the first pontiff to fly in an aeroplane and the first to leave Italy since Pope Pius IV in 1809, when he visits the Holy Land.

Jan 5th In China, Chairman Mao's *Little Red Book* is published. Officially called *Quotations From Chairman Mao Tse-Tung*, it quickly becomes a bestseller.

Jan 8th President Lyndon B. Johnson declares a 'War on Poverty'. He asks Congress to "work together to make this year's session the best in the nation's history... as the session which declared all-out war on human poverty and unemployment in these United States."

Jan 11th Young women of Britain, well some at least, go wild as the first issue of *Jackie* magazine hits the shelves. It offers a blend of fashion and beauty tips, gossip, short stories and comic strips.

Jan 20th Eleven men go on trial at Buckinghamshire Assizes in Aylesbury charged with offences relating to The Great Train Robbery of the previous year.

Jan 25th Blue Ribbon Sports is founded in Eugene, Oregon.

Feb 1st The Beatles take the number one spot in the American charts for the first time with *I Want To Hold Your Hand*.

Feb 3rd The Warren Commission begins its first hearings in the investigation of the murder of President John F. Kennedy. The first witness is Marina Oswald, widow of accused assassin Lee Harvey Oswald.

Feb 6th The British and French governments reach a deal to construct a twin tunnelled rail link under the Channel. It is expected to take six years to build.

Feb 7th   Beatlemania is in full flow in America. An appearance by the Fab Four on *The Ed Sullivan Show* breaks US television ratings records.

Feb 7th   The American detective series *77 Sunset Strip*, which had fired all of its original cast barring Efrem Zimbalist Jr., is pulled from ABC's schedules half way through its sixth season as ratings have plummeted.

Feb 10th   Sierra Leone becomes the first country in the world to introduce self-adhesive postage stamps, much to the annoyance of philatelists as the stamps are difficult to keep in mint condition when removing from letters .

Feb 11th   The port of Southampton is granted city status by royal charter. It is the first to be awarded under the reign of Queen Elizabeth II.

Feb 13th   It's Chinese New Year. Those born after this date fall under the Year of the Dragon and are strong, silent types with great leadership qualities. Those born before are Water Rabbits, filled with kindness and hope.

Feb 19th   Former goon Peter Sellers marries Swedish actress Britt Ekland in a ceremony in London.

Feb 21st   £10 notes are issued for the fist time in the UK since the Second World War. Most people will be lucky to get one, as government figures show that the average weekly wage is £16.

Feb 29th   All 75 passengers and 8 crew are lost as a Bristol Britannia 312 aircraft crashes into a mountainside near Innsbruck, Austria. Most of the people on-board were on their way to watch the Winter Olympics.

Mar 6th   Elizabeth Taylor is granted a decree absolute as she divorces her fourth husband, American entertainer Eddie Fisher.

Mar 10th   The Queen gives birth to her fourth child and third son who is named Edward Antony Richard Louis Windsor.

Mar 13th   After tucking in to a double cheeseburger, fries and a donut, diners can save on the calories by treating themselves to a diet Pepsi, as the first sugar free cola is launched in America.

Mar 14ᵗʰ　In the US, Billboard magazine reports that sales of Beatles records make up 60% of the entire singles market.

Mar 15ᵗʰ　Is it fifth time lucky for Elizabeth Taylor as she says "I do" and makes Richard Burton husband number five?

Mar 18ᵗʰ　A representative of the National Coal Board writes to a Merthyr Tydfil waterworks engineer stating that he "would not like to continue beyond the next 6/8 weeks in tipping coal slurry on Tip No. 7 at Aberfan where it is likely to be a source of danger to Pantglas school".

Mar 19ᵗʰ　Concrete cows and roundabouts are on the horizon as the government announces the creation of a new town to surround the village of Milton Keynes in north Buckinghamshire.

Mar 21ˢᵗ　The Eurovision Song Contest is broadcast live to over 100 million homes around Europe, from the Tivoli Concert Hall in Copenhagen. Italian Gigliola Cinquetti wins with her song *Non ho l'età*.

Mar 27ᵗʰ　An earthquake measuring 9.2 on the Richter scale strikes Alaska. Ground fissures, falling buildings and tsunamis resulting from the quake leave over 130 dead and cause millions of dollars worth of damage.

Mar 29ᵗʰ　The first purpose built Sikh Temple (Gurdwara) in Britain opens in Bradford. It is named after the seventeenth century poet, warrior and philosopher Guru Gobind Singh.

Apr 4ᵗʰ　The Beatles occupy the top five positions in the Billboard Top 100 chart. In order the songs are *Can't Buy Me Love, Twist and Shout, She Loves You, I Want to Hold Your Hand* and *Please Please Me*.

Apr 10ᵗʰ　David Threlfall, a 20-year-old sci-fi fan, bets £10 with bookmakers William Hill that "any man, woman or child, from any nation on Earth, being on the Moon, or any other planet, star or heavenly body of comparable distance from Earth, before January 1971." He is given out of this world odds of of 1,000 to 1.

Apr 12ᵗʰ　The London tabloid newspaper, The People, publishes a story titled: "The

Biggest Sports Scandal of the Century". They have uncovered the fact that three Sheffield Wednesday footballers had bet on their side to lose against Ipswich Town in a match on 1st December 1962. They duly lost 2-0 and the trio netted £100 profit.

Apr 13th Ian Smith is elected as the new leader of the Rhodesian Front and becomes the country's new Prime Minister. He stood on a mandate of independence from Britain and establishing white-minority rule.

Apr 13th Sidney Poitier scoops the best actor award at the Oscars for his lead role in *Lilies of the Field*. Patricia Neal is voted best actress for *Hud* and the Tony Richardson directed *Tom Jones* is named best film.

Apr 17th During a press conference on the White House lawn, President Lyndon Johnson decides to give members of the media an impromptu demonstration of how he could lift his two pet beagles by their ears, making them yowl. When questioned why he had done that, Johnson responded that it was "good for the dogs". Experts on handling dogs are quick to point out that Johnson must have been misinformed about the benefits to beagles by being lifted up by their ears.

Apr 20th Spread the word. The first jars of Nutella leave the Ferrero factory in Italy.

May 2nd West Ham United lift the F.A. Cup by beating Preston North End 3-2. Geoff Hurst scores the second goal for the Hammers, whilst Bobby Moore is steady in defence. We wonder if the pair will win anything else?

May 7th Students in Wakefield College, England attempt to set a record for the most people piled in one bed. Hoping to make it to 50 in a bed, they almost make it. But when they reach 47, a student at the bottom of the pile passes out with blood gushing from his nose. Note for the future: build a bigger bed.

May 11th Say goodbye to shabby tat. Terence Conran opens Habitat, the first fashionable interiors store. It is to be found on Fulham Road, Chelsea.

May 12th Briton, Elizabeth Alice Kensley celebrates her 109th birthday and is verified as the oldest person in the world. She was born during the Crimean War.

May 15ᵗʰ   An outbreak of typhoid in Aberdeen leads to hundreds falling ill and three people dying. The outbreak of the bacterial disease is traced to a single tin of corned beef being sold in a shop which didn't wash its knives between serving customers.

May 17ᵗʰ   Anyone for a tray of multi-coloured donuts? The first Tim Hortons, founded by the great Canadian ice hockey player of the same name, opens in Hamilton, Ontario and they are an immediate slam dunk. (wrong sport, ed)

May 23ʳᵈ   Dale Greig from Paisley runs the Isle of Wight marathon. The only problem is that Dale is a woman and women are not allowed to enter. Organisers get round the rules by letting her start ahead of the field, so she is not officially part of the race. She finishes in a world's best time of 3 hours 27 minutes and 25 seconds.

May 27ᵗʰ   Jawaharlal 'Pandit' Nehru, India's first post-independence Prime Minister dies.

Jun 4ᵗʰ   The failing Rolls Razor company is found to be overdrawn by £485,000. This is after managing director James Bloom persuades the board to pay out over £200,000 in dividends. A 'bloomin' cheek if you ask us.

Jun 6ᵗʰ   "Pardon me boys". Southern Railway 4501 is taken to Chattanooga, Tennessee for restoration by the Tennessee Valley Railroad Museum.

Jun 6ᵗʰ   The Rolling Stones are introduced to the American public in the pre-recorded TV show *The Hollywood Palace*. They sing *I Just Want to Make Love to You*. Host Dean Martin is not impressed, making a series of derogatory remarks including: "Their hair is not long. It's just smaller foreheads and higher eyebrows."

Jun 11ᵗʰ   Walter Seifert, a resident of Volkhoven, a suburb of Cologne attacks a Roman Catholic school with a home-made flamethrower shouting "Hitler the Second has returned." He kills ten and injures another 21 before his fuel runs out. He is then shot dead by police.

Jun 12ᵗʰ   At a Pretoria court Nelson Mandela is sentenced to life imprisonment for

acting against the Apartheid state of South Africa.

Jun 13th Graduate of the London Academy of Music and Dramatic Arts, Malcolm McDowell, lands his first television acting job in the soap opera *Crossroads*.

Jun 14th More than a hundred fans of The Beatles require hospital treatment for injuries in a crush when a quarter of a million people turn out to welcome the Fab Four on their first visit to Australia.

Jun 24th The annual Calcio storico fiorentino final takes place in Italy. It is an early form of football which dates back to the middle ages. The modern version of calcio has not changed much from its historical roots, which allow tactics such as head-butting, punching, elbowing and choking.

Jun 27th Actor, Ernest Borgnine and musical star Ethel Merman, promise "to have and to hold from this day forward, for better, for worse, for richer, for poorer, in sickness and in health, to love and to cherish, till death us do part", in another big show business marriage.

Jul 4th In an all-Australian final, Roy Emerson beats Fred Stolle in four sets to take the Wimbledon Men's Singles title.

Jul 7th Art is brought to the masses as Ole Christensen opens the first Athena poster shop on Hampstead High Street, London.

Jul 15th The Post Office Tower in London is topped out (meaning that the last beam has been laid).

Jul 20th Dorothy Podber, a photographer, is invited to Andy Warhol's Factory art studio. She asks if she can shoot his prints of Marilyn Monroe. Warhol consents. She then produces a gun and fires into them. Our advice to Andy is bin them and start again, but what do we know!

Jul 29th After their honeymoon both Ernest Borgnine and Ethel Merman decide that they really dislike each other and file for divorce.

Aug 2nd A crowd of some 16,000 turn up to see The Rolling Stones in Wiltshire. Lord Bath introduces the band at Longleat House, his stately home.

Aug 2nd   America is drawn further into the conflict between North and South Vietnam when US amphibious forces carrying out covert surveillance in the Gulf of Tonkin are attacked by North Vietnamese forces.

Aug 8th   Josie Hannon Fitzgerald, the maternal grandmother of John F. Kennedy, dies aged 98. News of her grandson's assassination has been withheld from her, for fear that the shock would be too much for her.

Aug 10th   At the International Congress of Psychiatrists in London, Dr. Milton Berger presents a paper in which he suggests that a baby's burps might be predictive of its personality and future success in life. A baby with "strong and clear" burps, he said, was likely to grow up to become a leader. However, a baby with soft "dithering" burps would be a nobody.

Aug 10th   In America, The "Gulf of Tonkin Resolution", formally known as "A Joint Resolution" to promote the maintenance of international peace and security in south-east Asia, is enacted. It is anything but, as it allows the US President to unilaterally declare war on another nation.

Aug 13th   NASA Astronauts Frank Borman, Neil Armstrong, John Young, and Deke Slayton, endure desert survival training in Reno, Nevada. Will any of them make 'one small step for man'?

Aug 15th   Fred 'Fiery' Trueman takes his 300th test wicket against Australia in the fifth test match at the Oval. He becomes the first bowler to take 300 wickets in test history.

Aug 22nd   *Match of the Day* makes its debut. An estimated TV audience of 20,000 tunes in to see highlights of Liverpool's 3-2 victory over Arsenal. This is fewer than half the number who watched the game live.

Sep 3rd   Joy fills the hearts of every numerically challenged school pupil as work starts on the Nuffield Mathematics Project. The team divide maths learning into five core subjects: Computation and Structure, Shape and Size, Graphs Leading to Algebra, Logic and Probability, and Statistics.

Sep 4th   The Forth Road Bridge opens to traffic, spanning the Firth of the Forth and linking South Queensferry, Edinburgh to Fife.

Sep 4th   The shortest session in the history of the United States Senate (two seconds) takes place. Senator Lee Metcalf of Montana calls the Senate to order and utters the words, "Under the previous order the Senate stands adjourned until Tuesday noon next" and he strikes the gavel. Try saying that in two seconds.

Sep 11th   The Beatles perform at the Gator Bowl in Jacksonville, Florida. When the venue was booked, the band was not aware that it was a segregated venue. After much negotiation, the organisers relented and the band played to a mixed audience.

Sep 14th   Pop Tarts hit the shelves in America. For Kellogg's, the 'slam-in-the-toaster and get the kids ready for school breakfast' is an instant hit.

Sep 15th   The Sun Newspaper launches as a broadsheet. It is aimed at a sophisticated and superior middle class, hitherto undetected and yearning for its own newspaper. How did that work out?

Oct 4th   Dublin beat Antrim 7-4 to 3-1 in the All-Ireland Senior Camogie Championship Final, held at Croke park in Dublin. Never heard of the sport? It is worth looking up, it is even mentioned in Samuel Beckett's play *Waiting for Godot*.

Oct 5th   Queen Elizabeth II begins a week-long state visit to Canada. It is to be her only visit to a Commonwealth country this year.

Oct 10th   In a moving opening ceremony at the Summer Olympics in Tokyo, the Olympic Flame is carried into the stadium by Yoshinori Sakai, who was born on 6th August 1945, the day the atom bomb was dropped on Hiroshima.

Oct 14th   It is announced that Martin Luther King Jr. is to be awarded the Nobel Peace Prize "for his non-violent struggle for civil rights for the Afro-American population."

Oct 17th   Prime Minister Harold Wilson appoints his first cabinet. Members include Jim Callaghan (who Wilson defeated in the party election of 1963), Barbara Castle, Dennis Healey and Roy Jenkins.

Oct 14th   American Bob Hayes becomes the first man to run the 100m in under ten seconds at the Olympic Games in Tokyo. Celebrations are cut short as the tailwind speed of 5.28m/s meant this run was ineligible for record purposes.

Oct 24th   Zambia, formerly Northern Rhodesia, gains independence from Great Britain. They make the announcement on the last day of the Olympics and become the only country to start a games with one name and leave it with another.

Oct 24th   The Tokyo Olympics draw to a close with America topping the medals table with 36 golds, but not if you read Russian newspapers. They have their athletes on top by virtue of winning more medals overall. (96 to America's 90).

Oct 30th   The satirical magazine *Private Eye* carries a picture of the Queen at the State Opening of Parliament, accompanied by a speech bubble stating "…and I hope you realise I didn't write this crap."

Nov 2nd   The soap opera *Crossroads* bursts onto our screens, but hopefully not too forcefully as the sets seem to be made of plywood.

Nov 3rd   As the results come in from around the states in the US Presidential election, all signs point to a resounding win for the incumbent, Lyndon B. Johnson, over his Republican rival Barry Goldwater. The democrats also widen their majorities in both houses.

Nov 8th   The opening ceremony of the 2nd Summer Paralympics takes place. 369 athletes from 22 countries take part in the games. These include Dick Thompson who won four gold medals at the 1960 games.

Nov 9th   The UK Parliament votes to abolish the death penalty for murder in Britain. Too late for Peter Anthony Allen and Gwynne Owen, who on 14th August 1964 were the last people to be hanged for their part in the murder of John Alan West in Cumbria.

Nov 10th   Prime Minister Wilson's government survives a vote of no confidence. The motion, which failed 294 to 315, is over the Labour government's plans for

free health care, larger pensions and higher taxes "to take from citizens according to their means, to give to citizens according to their means."

Nov 12ᵗʰ The Paralympics draw to a close. The United States top the medals table with 50 golds, Britain comes second with 18.

Nov 12ᵗʰ Members of the ultra leftist Zengakuren students association in Japan drag and beat a policeman during a protest demonstration at Sasebo naval base, against the arrival of the US nuclear-powered submarine Sea Dragon.

Dec 1ˢᵗ The board game *Dodge the Daleks* hits the shelves. Cashing in on the *Doctor Who* craze, the game involves players having to, surprise surprise, dodge the Daleks. And yes it is basically a bad form of ludo but with better pieces.

Dec 3ʳᵈ Sirimavo Bandaranaike, the world's first elected woman Prime Minister, is voted out of office in a narrow 74-73 vote in the parliament in Ceylon.

Dec 10ᵗʰ Dorothy Hodgkin receives the Nobel Prize in Chemistry at a ceremony in Stockholm.

Dec 12ᵗʰ *The Guinness Book of Records* sells its millionth copy. Some kind of record?

Dec 17ᵗʰ In the UK, the government passes an act to put Britain's nuclear arsenal under NATO control. The debate is heated and the measure passes by 311 to 291. Prime Minister, Harold Wilson, counters the argument of the opposition by asking "Are you willing to go it alone in a war with Russia? Would you push the button setting off a kind of war that would mean total annihilation of all human life in Britain? If you can't answer that, you don't understand what the argument is all about."

Dec 23ʳᵈ Dr. Beeching leaves his job to join ICI, following the publication of his report 'The Reshaping of British Railways' in 1963. More than 8,000 miles of track and 2,000 stations were closed at a cost of nearly 70,000 jobs.

Dec 25ᵗʰ Children around the country excitedly open their Christmas presents. Many are hoping for this year's craze, a Booma Boomerang…we wonder if the company offered returns.

Jeffrey Preston Bezos born Jeffrey Preston Jorgensen
born on 12th January 1964 in Albuquerque, New Mexico, USA

Bezos is an American entrepreneur and founder of Amazon. His mother Jacklyn, was a Danish-American unicyclist and his father struggled financially largely through his love for the bottle. His mother filed for divorce when Jeff was just 17 months old. She then married Cuban Miguel 'Mike' Bezos in 1968 and changed her son's name. Bezos started Amazon in 1994 as an online bookstore and transformed it into one of the world's largest and most influential e-commerce and technology companies. His vision extended beyond retail, leading Amazon to diversify into cloud computing, artificial intelligence, streaming services and more. Under his leadership, Amazon became synonymous with innovation, disrupting traditional retail and reshaping industries. He is known for his relentless focus on customer satisfaction and long-term thinking. His leadership principles, outlined in Amazon's philosophy, emphasise innovation, frugality and a commitment to long-term success. In 2021, Bezos stepped down as Amazon's CEO allowing him to focus on other ventures, including his space exploration company, Blue Origin. Bezos is one of the richest people in the world, and his impact on the business and technology landscape is profound.

Bezos summed up his work philosophy when he said. "If you can't feed a team with two pizzas, its too large." He clearly believes that small is beautiful, but that the sum of these parts makes big beautiful as well.

Michelle LaVaughn Robinson Obama
born on 17th January 1964 in Chicago, Illinois, USA

Michelle is a lawyer, writer and advocate who served as the First Lady of the United States from 2009 to 2017. She grew up in Chicago and attended Princeton University and Harvard Law School. After graduating, she worked as a lawyer in Chicago where she met Barack Obama, whom she married in 1992. Michelle subsequently served as an assistant to the mayor of Chicago and then as the assistant commissioner of planning and development for the city. During her time as First Lady, she became a prominent advocate for various causes, including education, health and military families. She launched several initiatives such as Let's Move!, aimed at combating childhood obesity, and Joining Forces, which supported service members, veterans and their families. Beyond her policy initiatives, she also became known for her advocacy for women and girls, delivering speeches and participating in campaigns worldwide. She is an accomplished author, penning the bestselling memoir *Becoming*, in which she shares her personal journey, challenges and experiences as First Lady. Michelle Obama's impact extends far beyond her years in the White House. She continues to be an influential figure, inspiring people globally through her advocacy work, writing, and public speaking engagements.

"Let's be very clear: Strong men - men who are truly role models - don't need to put down women to make themselves feel powerful. People who are truly strong lift others up. People who are truly powerful bring others together."

Barbara Jane Horrocks
born on 18th January 1964 in Rawtenstall, Lancashire, UK

Horrocks trained at The Royal Academy of Dramatic Art, alongside Imogen Stubbs and Ralph Fiennes, before moving to the Royal Shakespeare Company. 1992 saw her land the role of Bubble, the ditzy assistant to Jennifer Saunder's Edina in *Absolutely Fabulous*. Her breakout starring role was in the 1998 film *Little Voice*, where her astonishing portrayal of a timid and introverted character with a remarkable singing voice garnered critical acclaim and catapulted her to stardom. She has appeared in numerous stage productions including *Cabaret*, *The Rise and Fall of Little Voice* and *Annie Get Your Gun*, further cementing her reputation as a versatile and talented performer. Proving herself adept at playing in hard-hitting dramas she has often worked with director Mike Leigh in such films as *Life Is Sweet* and *Career Girls*. She is an excellent mimic and in 2000 produced an album of duets with, among others, Dean Martin and Robbie Williams, singing in the various styles of her favourite divas. Horrocks' distinctive voice has also featured in animated films such as *Chicken Run* and *Arthur Christmas*. Her ability to seamlessly transition between different mediums and genres is a testament to her tremendous skill and range as an artist.

"When I think of Marilyn Monroe, and achieving her sound, I think of having a rather large bust. I think of her physically and I am just able to create her sound, because her physicality was so much to do with her sound."

Eleanor Nancy Macpherson
born on 29th March 1964 in Killara, New South Wales, Australia

Macpherson is a renowned model, businesswoman and actress. Widely recognised for her striking beauty and towering stature, she earned the nickname 'The Body' during her successful modelling career in the 1980s and 1990s. Her career began in 1982 with a television commercial for Tab (an early diet coca-cola) which established her as a 'girl next door' figure in Australia. Her big breakthrough came when she appeared on the cover of the Sports Illustrated Swimsuit Issue in the 1980s, catapulting her to international fame. Her tall, athletic figure and stunning looks made her a sought-after model for top fashion brands and magazines. Over the years, she graced numerous magazine covers and walked the runways for prestigious designers, solidifying her status as one of the world's most iconic supermodels. Beyond modelling, Macpherson expanded her career into acting, appearing in films such as *Sirens* and *The Edge* and on TV, most notably as Joey's new room-mate in *Friends*. She also ventured into business, establishing a successful lingerie line called Elle Macpherson Intimates. Her entrepreneurial spirit further led her to co-found WelleCo, a wellness and nutrition company. Elle Macpherson's enduring success in the fashion industry, coupled with her business acumen, has made her a multifaceted and influential figure.

In 1995, along with Naomi Campbell, Claudia Schiffer and Christy Turlington, Macpherson opened the Fashion Cafe in New York. Unfortunately, the venture was only short lived due to poor management.

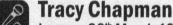 Tracy Chapman
born on 30th March 1964 in Cleveland, Ohio, USA

At the age of 24, Chapman burst onto the folk music scene, captivating audiences worldwide. Her impact extends far beyond her remarkable success as a multi-platinum, four-time Grammy Award-winning artist. Chapman redefined protest music, infusing her anthems with personal experiences that resonate deeply. Raised in Cleveland, Ohio, Chapman was a quiet child, often found immersed in books at the local library. It wasn't until her university days that her musical talents were discovered while she was out busking. Her iconic track *Talkin' Bout A Revolution* became a generational protest anthem, following in the footsteps of Bob Dylan. Her versatile artistry includes poignant storytelling with hits like *Fast Car*. Her emotional depth was further showcased in *Baby Can I Hold You Tonight*, which she famously once performed alongside Luciano Pavarotti. Beyond music, Chapman is a dedicated social activist, lending her voice to causes like Amnesty International, AIDS/ LifeCycle, and the anti-Apartheid movement in South Africa. In recognition of her unwavering support and friendship towards South Africa, Chapman was honoured with the National Order of the Companions of O.R. Tambo on 16th April 2023. This prestigious award acknowledges distinguished foreign individuals who have demonstrated exceptional solidarity with South Africa.

Chapman secured a spot in Nelson Mandela's 70th birthday tribute concert when, by chance, the star performer Stevie Wonder dropped out. Prior to the concert, she had sold 250,000 albums. In the fortnight afterwards, she sold two million.

Andrew Clement Serkis
born on 20th April 1964 in Ruislip Manor, Middlesex, UK

Andy Serkis is a highly acclaimed English actor, director and producer. He is renowned for his groundbreaking work in motion capture technology, bringing iconic characters to life in films like *The Lord of the Rings* trilogy, where he portrayed Gollum. His ability to convey nuanced emotions through digital characters earned him widespread recognition and paved the way for the acceptance of motion capture as a legitimate form of acting. In addition to Gollum, Serkis played pivotal roles in other blockbuster franchises, including Caesar in the *Planet of the Apes* series and Supreme Leader Snoke in the *Star Wars* trilogy. His dedication to performance-capture extends beyond acting; he founded The Imaginarium Studios, a motion-capture and performance-capture studio showcasing his commitment to advancing cinematic technology. Apart from his contributions in front of the camera, Serkis has also directed films like *Breathe* and *Mowgli: Legend of the Jungle*. His directorial ventures highlight his versatility and passion for storytelling. Known for his transformative performances and technological contributions to the film industry, Andy Serkis continues to be a trailblazer in the realm of digital performance and film making.

Serkis sees his role as part of a long continuum of acting: "Greek Theatre started off and used masks, and Kabuki, in the East, they used mask-work. And then, Commedia dell'arte in Italy and then, you know, we're part of an acting tradition, and performance capture is no different."

 ### David Lionel Baddiel
born on 28th May 1964 in Troy, New York, USA

David Baddiel is a versatile entertainer, renowned for his talents as a comedian, author, screenwriter, and television host. His comedy career grew through hit TV shows like *The Mary Whitehouse Experience* and *Newman and Baddiel in Pieces*. In a groundbreaking moment in 1992, he and Rob Newman performed to a crowd of 12,500 at Wembley Arena, marking the UK's first arena comedy show. Collaborating with Frank Skinner, Baddiel co-created and presented fan-favourites such as *Fantasy Football* and *Baddiel & Skinner Unplanned*. Together with The Lightning Seeds, they penned the iconic football anthem *Three Lions*. Beyond comedy, Baddiel's repertoire extends to acclaimed documentaries, from his travel memoir *David Baddiel On The Silk Road* to his recent groundbreaking work *Confronting Holocaust Denial*. He's also made a mark in children's literature with bestsellers like *The Boy Who Got Accidentally Famous* and *The Boy Who Could Do What He Liked*. His Sunday Times bestselling nonfiction book *Jews Don't Count* won critical acclaim, spawning a documentary of the same title. In the realm of fiction, Baddiel has crafted compelling adult novels like *The Death of Eli Gold* and *Time For Bed*, alongside scripting the popular comedy film *The Infidel*. Additionally, he's been a creative force in radio, creating and starring in recurring shows like *Heresy* and *Don't Make Me Laugh*.

Baddiel has long suffered and publicly documented his battle with insomnia.

 ### Katherine 'Kathy' Lucy Bridget Burke
born on 13th June 1964 in Islington, Greater London, UK

Actor and borderline national treasure Kathy Burke was a feature of British stage and screen until 2004, when she fell out of love with acting and all but retired, only popping up occasionally in minor roles such as playing Connie Sachs in the film *Tinker, Tailor, Soldier, Spy* (2011). What she left was a great legacy in both serious and comedic acting. Her mother died when she was just 18 months old so she has no memory of her being around. 'Our Kaff's' career took off when she appeared in a series of great films in which she gave outstanding performances. Most notably *Nil by Mouth*, for which she won the Prix d'interprétation féminine (Best Actress Award) at the 1997 Cannes Film Festival. On the small screen, she is probably best known for her comic characters such as Linda La Hughes in *Gimme, Gimme, Gimme* and starring alongside Harry Enfield in *Harry Enfield's Television Programme*. To this day, quotes from her iconic characters Perry and Waynetta Slob are still quoted. Kathy has also played royalty twice. She was Queen Mary in the Oscar-winning film *Elizabeth* alongside Cate Blanchett and played the Queen Mother in *PsychoBitches* on TV.

In 1997 Burke introduced a young unknown film-maker, Joe Wright, to Gary Oldman at a private viewing of *Nil By Mouth*. Oldman asked her if Wright was any good. Burke replied "Give it a few years and he'll direct you in a film that will win you an Oscar." In 2018 he did, for the film *Darkest Hour*.

Alexander Boris de Pfeffel Johnson
born on 19ᵗʰ June 1964 in New York City, USA

Johnson, is a British politician who has played a prominent role in UK politics. Known for his distinctive appearance, including a dishevelled blond hairstyle, he is a charismatic and unconventional figure and has had a multifaceted career. Before entering politics, he pursued a career in journalism and served as the editor of The Spectator. He was elected as the MP for Henley in 2001. Later he became the Mayor of London in 2008, a position he held for two terms until 2016; a remarkable achievement in a left-leaning city. As a prominent member of the Conservative Party, Johnson successfully campaigned for the 'Leave' side in the 2016 Brexit referendum. After Theresa May's resignation, he became the leader of the Conservative Party and subsequently the Prime Minister of the United Kingdom in July 2019. Johnson's premiership was marked by significant events, most notably the challenges posed by the COVID-19 pandemic (he himself landed up in intensive care after catching the virus). D'Israeli described becoming Prime Minister as "reaching the top of a greasy pole". Johnson slid down it all too quickly. After delivering a landslide victory for his party in the December 2019 general election, things began to go wrong. Lockdown violating parties were held at Downing Street and other scandals involving lobbying and inappropriate behaviour blind-sided him. By-election defeats and mass resignations from the cabinet followed and on 7ᵗʰ July 2022, Johnson resigned saying "hasta la vista baby."

"My policy on cake is pro having it and pro eating it."

Sandra Annette Bullock
born on 26ᵗʰ July 1964 in Arlington County, Virginia, USA

Bullock comes from a family steeped in performance art. Her mother was an opera singer and her father a voice coach. She is known for her versatility and charismatic on-screen presence. With a career spanning several decades, she has become one of Hollywood's most bankable stars. She gained widespread recognition in the 1990s with roles in films like *Speed* (1994), where her dynamic performance opposite Keanu Reeves showcased her ability to carry action-packed blockbusters. Bullock's talent extends beyond action, as evidenced by her Academy Award-winning role in the drama *The Blind Side* (2009), where she portrayed, a strong-willed woman who rescues a homeless teenager. Known for her down-to-earth persona, she has a diverse filmography that includes romantic comedies like *While You Were Sleeping* (1995) and *Miss Congeniality* (2000), as well as critically acclaimed dramas such as *Crash* (2004) and *Gravity* (2013). More recent she gave a critically acclaimed performance in the Netflix post-apocalyptic horror film *Bird Box* (2018). She has also ventured into producing, demonstrating her commitment to shaping compelling narratives in the entertainment industry. Off-screen, she is recognised for her philanthropic efforts and has actively supported various charitable causes.

In 2014, Bullock designed a space-themed Paddington Bear statue which she called 'Gravity Bear' in homage to the 2013 film *Gravity*. Fifty were placed around London in various locations and were later auctioned to raise money for children's charities.

Jürgen Klinsmann
born on 30ᵗʰ July 1964 in Göppingen, West Germany

Klinsmann was born into a family of bakers and is a journeyman baker by trade. He can also be described as a journeyman footballer as he has plied his trade in Germany, Italy, England and America, learning languages, scoring goals and delighting fans wherever he went. In sport the term journeyman has become somewhat devalued. Klinsmann is closer to its true meaning: someone who can take their expertise into any situation. After a successful stint at AFB Stuttgart (79 goals in 156 appearances), he left for Inter Milan where he helped them to UEFA Cup glory. Next was AS Monaco but injury affected his time there. He then moved to Tottenham Hotspur in 1994, but his reputation as someone who went to ground too easily preceded him. On his debut against Sheffield Wednesday, he scored the winning header and immediately won over fans with his celebration by self-mockingly diving to the ground. A Guardian journalist who had written an article called "Why I Hate Jürgen Klinsmann", wrote another two months later titled "Why I Love Jürgen Klinsmann". Klinsmann went on to win the 1995 Football Writers' Player of the Year Award. In 1995 he returned to his homeland, this time playing for the mighty Bayern Munich. His trophy cabinet includes domestic titles, European trophies a coveted World Cup winner's medal.

When Klinsmann lived in London, he drove around in a Volkswagen beetle. Although he was instantly recognisable, he perfected a cockney accent, saying "yeah, I do look a bit like 'im" allowing him to go around in relative peace.

Keanu Charles Reeves
born on 2ⁿᵈ September 1964 in Beirut, Lebanon

Reeves is an actor, producer and musician. After small roles in *Youngblood* (1986) and *Dangerous Liaisons* (1988), he then starred as Ted 'Theodore' Logan in the riotously funny *Bill and Ted's Excellent Adventure* alongside Alex Winter. The film popularised the word bodacious, which far from being new first appeared in print around 1800. Reeves went on to gain widespread recognition for his roles in iconic films such as *The Matrix* trilogy, where he portrayed the stoic and enigmatic character Neo. In the *John Wick* film series, he showcased his skill in intense action sequences. Beyond acting, he has also played bass guitar in the alternative rock band Dogstar (1991-2002) and in 1995 they were the supporting band for David Bowie at the Hollywood Bowl. Reeves' versatility as an actor has allowed him to tackle a range of roles, from action-packed blockbusters, to comedy, to more introspective and dramatic films. His enduring popularity is not only attributable to his talent but also to his authenticity. He has earned respect from both colleagues and fans all over the world. Outside of the successful franchises he has worked on, he has been kept busy buy doing voice-overs and video game work, most recently in the *Toy Story* animated series and the *Cyberpunk 2077* series of video games.

Keanu means 'cool breeze over the mountain in Hawaiian.' During his early acting career his agent thought his name was too exotic. He is sometimes credited as K.C. Reeves, Norman Kreeves or Chuck Spadina.

 ## Susie Dent
born on 21st September 1964 in Woking, Surrey, UK

Susie Dent, a lexicographer and etymologist, is renowned for her long-standing role in 'Dictionary Corner' on Channel 4's *Countdown* since 1992. Since 2016, she has been the Honorary Vice-President of the Chartered Institute of Editing and Proofreading. Additionally, Dent co-hosts the podcast *Something Rhymes With Purple* with Gyles Brandreth, launched in 2019. She attended the Marist Convent in Ascot, an independent Roman Catholic day school and briefly studied at Eton College to prepare for Oxbridge entrance exams. Subsequently, she pursued her BA in modern languages at Somerville College, Oxford followed by a master's degree in German at Princeton University. Susie developed a passion for words from a young age. On family trips, while her sister read magazines, she immersed herself in German or French vocabulary books, eagerly learning new words before reaching their destination. She is famed for her 'Word of the Day' which she publishes online, bringing obscure words back to life. They are often topical, as with 'ingordigiousness': extreme greed; an insatiable desire for wealth at any cost. So we thought we would have a go. She is definitely not a 'sciolist' [1], or a 'blatherskite' [2], although she has been known to 'divagate' [3] and she is certainly a 'snoutfair' [4].

[1] a person who pretends to be knowledgeable. [2] a person who talks at great length without making much sense. [3] to stray or wander off the subject. [4] a good-looking person.

 ## Matthew Keith Hall aka Harry Hill
born on 1st October 1964 in Woking, Surrey, UK

Harry Hill was born in Woking, Surrey. He spent his early years in Kent and then lived as a teenager in Hong Kong. He trained as a doctor, holds a medical degree from the University of London and is still registered as a medical practitioner. He made his comedy debut at the Edinburgh Fringe in 1992, winning the Perrier best newcomer prize. It lead to comedy series for BBC Two and Channel 4, before he created *Harry Hill's TV Burp* for ITV, which ran for 11 years from 2001. More recently he created *Harry Hill's Alien Fun Capsule*, two series of *Harry Hill's Tea-Time* and *Harry Hill's World of TV*. He is the long-standing voice of ITV's *You've Been Framed* and is the co-host of Channel 4's *Junior Bake Off*. He has written several joke books, the children's novel series *Matt Millz* and the autobiography, *Fight: Thirty Years Not Quite At The Top*. He is also an accomplished artist and has shown his work at the Royal Academy. In 2022, Hill joined the judging panel at Art of London, a project run by National Gallery X and King's College London to select up-and-coming artists, who were commissioned to splash vivid, optimistic images throughout a trail across the West End.

"I knew I was going bald when it started to take longer and longer to wash my face".

"My aunt used to say, 'What you can't see, can't hurt you'...well, she died of radiation poisoning a few months back!"

 ### Clive Owen
born on 3rd October 1964 in Keresley, Warwickshire, UK

Owen is one of only a handful of actors who can switch his talents from art house cinema to mainstream movies. Acting was not his first choice as a profession, but he changed his mind and went on to graduate from the Royal Academy of Dramatic Arts in 1987. He then joined the Young Vic Theatre Company performing in a number of Shakespearean productions. He became a fully-fledged TV star playing devilish rogue Stephen Crane in *Chancer* in 1990. However, the now-sought-after actor abandoned the star-making part at the height of the show's popularity because of unwanted invasion of privacy and his fear of typecasting. In 1991, he played a brother caught in an incestuous relationship with his sister in Stephen Poliakoff's *Close My Eyes*. It has been the most controversial role of his acting career. In 1993, Owen acted in his first American film *Class of 61*, a war movie in which he played the role of an Irish soldier. Owen was tipped to replace Pierce Brosnan as James Bond and was the public's favoured choice. It wasn't to be, but he did feature in the *The Bourne Identity* (2002). He starred alongside Bruce Willis and Mickey Rourke in the 2005 film *Sin City*. More recently he has played characters as diverse as Ernest Hemingway in *Hemingway and Gellhorn* (2012), Claudius in *Ophelia* (2018) and Bill Clinton in *American Crime Story* (2021).

Quote: "The sexiest part of the body is the eyes. That's what I believe." It is no coincidence that Owen has very nice eyes.

 ## Other Notable Births

 Nicholas Cage
7th January 1964
Actor | Producer

 Christopher Eccleston
16th February 1964
Actor

 Matt Dillon
18th February 1964
Actor

 Prince Edward
10th March 1964
British Royal

 Neneh Cherry
10th March 1964
Singer | Songwriter

 Rob Lowe
17th March 1964
Actor | Filmmaker

 Lenny Kravitz
26th May 1964
Singer | Actor

 Courteney Cox
15th June 1964
Actress | Filmmaker

 David Morrissey
21st June 1964
Actor | Filmmaker

 Ross Kemp
21st July 1964
Actor | Presenter

 Bonnie Langford
22nd July 1964
Actress | Dancer

 Sarah Lancashire
10th October 1964
Actress

 Gregg Wallace
17th October 1964
Broadcaster | Writer

 Kamala Harris
20th October 1964
Politician | Attorney

 Famke Janssen
5th November 1964
Actress

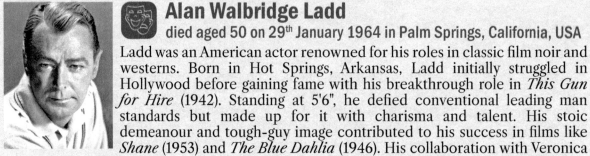

Alan Walbridge Ladd
died aged 50 on 29th January 1964 in Palm Springs, California, USA

Ladd was an American actor renowned for his roles in classic film noir and westerns. Born in Hot Springs, Arkansas, Ladd initially struggled in Hollywood before gaining fame with his breakthrough role in *This Gun for Hire* (1942). Standing at 5'6", he defied conventional leading man standards but made up for it with charisma and talent. His stoic demeanour and tough-guy image contributed to his success in films like *Shane* (1953) and *The Blue Dahlia* (1946). His collaboration with Veronica Lake in several films became iconic. His last role was as Nevada Smith in the film adaptation of Harold Robbins' *The Carpetbaggers*, which was released after his death. Despite personal challenges and a tragically short life, Alan Ladd left an indelible mark on cinema and is remembered for his performances and contributions to the golden age of Hollywood.

Nancy Astor born Nancy Witcher Langhorne
died aged 84 on 2nd May 1964 in Grimsthorpe Castle, Lincs, UK

Astor was a pioneering British politician who made history as the first woman to sit as an MP in the House of Commons. She entered politics in 1919, succeeding her husband as the Conservative MP for Plymouth Sutton after his elevation to the House of Lords. Astor's political career was marked by her advocacy of social and educational issues. Despite facing initial scepticism and resistance due to her gender, she went on to serve as an MP for over twenty-five years. She played a significant role in advancing women's rights and reshaping perceptions of women in politics during a transformative period in British history. During her time in Parliament, Astor was an advocate for temperance, welfare, education reforms and women's rights. She was also an ardent anti-Catholic and anti-communist, and received criticism for her anti-Semitism and sympathetic view of Nazism. Astor served in Parliament until 1945 when she was persuaded to step down, as her outspokenness made her a political liability in the final years of WWII.

Jawaharlal Nehru
died aged 74 on 27th May 1964 in New Delhi, India

Jawaharlal Nehru, often referred to as Pandit Nehru, was a pivotal figure in India's struggle for independence. He became its first Prime Minister. Born in, 1889, he belonged to a prominent political family. Nehru played a crucial role in shaping the destiny of post-independence India. His vision for a modern, secular and democratic nation guided the drafting of the Indian Constitution. Nehru's leadership emphasised economic development, industrialisation and the establishment of educational institutions. His commitment to social justice and secularism laid the foundation for a diverse and inclusive India. Despite facing challenges such as the partition of the country in 1947 and early economic struggles, Nehru's policies contributed to India's progress. He was a charismatic statesman, an eloquent speaker and an advocate for peace on the global stage. His daughter Indira Gandhi and his grandson Rajiv both became Prime Ministers. Both were victims of politically motivated murder.

Ian Lancaster Fleming

died aged 56 on 12th August 1964 in Canterbury, Kent, UK

Ian Fleming was a British author best known for creating the iconic fictional spy, James Bond. Born in London, Fleming worked as a journalist and served in British Naval Intelligence during World War II, experiences that influenced his later writing. In 1953, he introduced James Bond in the novel *Casino Royale*, marking the beginning of a successful literary and cultural phenomenon. Fleming's Bond series, characterised by its suave protagonist, thrilling espionage plots and exotic locations, gained immense popularity. He wrote a total of 14 Bond novels before his death in 1964. Fleming's contribution to the spy genre and popular culture continues to endure through numerous film adaptations and the lasting legacy of the charismatic secret agent, James Bond. Of the James Bond films, he only saw *Dr. No* (1962) and *From Russia With Love* (1963) as finished films. He did however manage to get on the set of *Goldfinger* (1964) and see it being filmed.

Cole Albert Porter

died aged 73 on 15th October 1964 in Santa Monica California, USA

Porter was an American composer and songwriter known for his sophisticated and witty contributions to musical theatre and popular music. Born in Indiana, Porter displayed early musical talent and studied at Yale University. His prolific career spanned several decades, producing iconic songs such as *Night and Day*, *I've Got You Under My Skin* and *Anything Goes*. Porter's distinctive style blended catchy melodies with clever lyrics, earning him widespread acclaim. His Broadway successes include *Kiss Me, Kate* (an interpretation of Shakespeare's *The Taming of the Shrew*) and *Can-Can*, showcasing his flair for blending romance, humour and theatricality. Despite suffering a horse-riding accident that left him in chronic pain, Porter continued to compose leaving an indelible mark on American music. His timeless contributions remain celebrated in the realms of musical theatre and popular songwriting.

Portrait by Roger Fry

Edith Louisa Sitwell

died aged 77 on 9th December 1964 in London, England, UK

Dame Edith Sitwell was a prominent British poet, critic and eccentric literary figure of the 20th century. Renowned for her distinctive appearance, with elaborate clothing and large jewellery, she made a significant impact on the modernist literary scene. Her poetry, marked by its experimentation with form and language, often explored themes of alienation, war and the human condition. She was part of the influential literary group known as the 'Sitwells', alongside her brothers Osbert and Sacheverell, contributing to the cultural landscape of the early 1900s. Notable works include *Facade*, a collaboration with composer William Walton, and her autobiographical writings. Edith Sitwell's contributions to literature and her unapologetic individualism left an enduring legacy, influencing subsequent generations of writers and artists. She summed up her position in society when she stated "I am not eccentric. It's just that I am more alive than most people. I am an unpopular electric eel set in a pond of catfish."

The Coins We Used

7 years before decimalisation, the United Kingdom used the system of **pounds**, **shillings** and **pence**, commonly represented using the symbols **£sd**. The **£** symbol evolved over many years from the letter **L** which derives from the Latin word *libra*, meaning a pound of money. Although **s** is the first letter of the word shilling, the use of the letter derives from the Latin word *solidus*, which means coin. The curious use of the letter **d** for pennies also has a Latin origin from the word *denarius*, meaning containing ten.

Unlike the decimal system based on multiples of 10, the pre-decimal system was based on multiples of 12. There were 12 pennies to a shilling and 240 pennies to a pound. This meant there were 20 shillings to the pound. In 1964 there were 8 coins in circulation with evocative names that still permeate our language today. Note: The farthing (¼ d) ceased to be legal tender 3 years earlier in 1961.

Halfpenny ½ d *In use to 1969*	Commonly known as the *ha'penny* it is was the only word in the English language with a silent 'f'. Since 1937 the coin featured Sir Francis Drake's ship The Golden Hind. The popular pub game *Shove Ha'penny* features 5 halfpennies.
Penny 1d *In use to 1971*	Before 1860 the penny was a large copper coin. This is why bicycles with a large front wheel were nicknamed Penny Farthings. Popular expressions using the penny include *ten a penny* and *a penny for your thoughts*.
Threepence 3d *In use to 1971*	These 12-sided coins were commonly known as *thruppence* or *thrupenny bits*. The silver versions known as *joeys* were often hidden in Christmas puddings making an exciting find for the lucky children who discovered them.
Sixpence 6d *In use to 1980*	These silver coins reputedly brought good luck. Sixpences were placed in brides' shoes as a wedding gesture. Known as benders, they could easily be bent. *Going on a bender* derived from drinking all day in pubs with sixpence.
Shilling 1/- *In use to 1990*	First minted in the reign of Henry VII as a testoon, the shilling was latterly commonly known as a bob. *Taking the king's shilling* meant enrolling in the army whilst *a few bob short of a pound* describes someone a bit dim.
Florin 2/- *In use to 1992*	The florin was Britain's first decimal coin in response to calls in the mid 19th century for decimal coinage to be introduced. As 2 bob, the florin was worth 1/10th of a pound. After decimalisation in 1971, florins became worth 10 pence.
Half Crown 2/6 *In use to 1969*	Half crowns were originally struck in gold in the reign of Henry VIII. The first silver half crowns were issued under Edward VI in 1549. Surviving for over 450 years, the half crown was one of the most successful coins of all time.
Crown 5/- *In use to present day*	The British crown is a heavy silver coin. Rarely spent, crowns are often minted for commemorative purposes. After decimalisation a crown was worth 25p until 1990 when their face value was changed to £5.

The average annual wage in the UK in 1964 was approximately:

£850-£900

The Mark I Ford Cortina was launched in the UK in 1962. Originally to be named the Ford Consul 225, the car was launched as the Consul Cortina until a facelift in 1964 when the Consul name was dropped. The 50hp standard model would go from 0-60 in 22.5 seconds using its 1198 cc, 4 cylinder engine. Base model prices started at:

£600

The price of the average house would be approximately 3-5x the average annual wage. Depending on where you were in the country this meant the price of a typical 1930's 3-bedroom semi-detached house would be in the region of:

£2,500 - £3,000

The Olympia Splendid 33 portable manual typewriter cost:

£24

In 1964, the average cost for a pint of milk would have been:

8½d

A gallon of petrol (which is equivalent to 4.5 litres) cost:

5s

Working Overseas

"Ten Pound Poms" en route to Australia on-board SS New Australia

At work on a rubber plantation in Malaysia

The ten pound assisted passage scheme to Australia proved extremely popular, with two clear waves of migration occurring firstly in the immediate post-war period, and then peaking in the 1960s. These 'Ten Pound Poms', as they became known (82% were English), were mostly from an urban background and were motivated by various factors: to escape post-war austerity, to take advantage of a warmer climate and an outdoor lifestyle, or to fulfil a sense of adventure. Migrants were required to stay for two years, giving up their passports on arrival, able only to return to Britain if they paid back their outward fare in full, in addition to paying for their journey home. At the beginning of the period there was a focus on assisting migrants who had certain skill sets such as building tradesmen or nurses, but by the 1960s there was less emphasis placed on these requirements. A preference for married migrants under the age of 51 and for single migrants under 46 remained. Health checks were conducted to ensure applicants suffering from diseases such as tuberculosis were not accepted. Other overseas opportunities for women included working as an au pair, a governess or in teaching and academia. For men, there were roles in management in former colonies. One such role was to be found in the rubber plantations of Malaysia which gained independence from Britain in 1957.

Life on a Rubber Plantation: After an interview and upon acceptance, young men would sign up for anywhere between 4 and 7 years. The initial role was as trainee estate manager. Even though it afforded great privilege, it was not without hardship. For many it was their first time away from home comforts and family. They would have to learn how to tap rubber (though this would never be their job), speak Malay and get used to the sweltering heat which necessitated starting work at sunrise. Anyone who couldn't hack it would not only have to fund their own fare home, but in many cases would have to pay the company for their outward journey. This could lead to great financial hardship. If the trainee gained promotion to estate manager, they were afforded a driver and a housekeeper. Although they were masters of all they surveyed, they faced a difficult balancing act. Local Malays were employed as clearers of the jungle with Tamils (originally from Southern India) and Chinese employed as rubber tappers. Keeping everybody happy was a difficult juggling act, compounded by the fact that there was a Chinese communist led insurgency. There were shops on the estate where products from home could be bought at great expense. The savvy Brit soon learned to eat as locals did at a fraction of the cost. After work, there was always the club where ex-pats could mingle. Gin in the afternoon, whisky in the evening and settle the bill at the end of the month, was the general rule.

Women's Work

With the exception of the two World Wars when women filled jobs otherwise undertaken by men who were posted overseas, the role of women was little changed for decades. In the early 1960s things were about to change, but only very slowly. In 1963/4 only one quarter of university students studying in Great Britain were women. Even upon graduation things were still unequal. It was only in 1961 that legislation was passed giving women equal pay in the civil service. It wasn't until 1975 that it became illegal to sack a woman for being pregnant. Women could legally be refused service to spend their own money in a pub. This law didn't change until 1982. Women who had gained equal suffrage with men in 1928 increasingly

Women mostly occupied administrative roles

began to demand a right to a proper education, equal pay and affordable childcare. But for most women their work would be in the home. It would start with making breakfast for the whole family, then making sure that the husband was suitably attired for work and that the children were ready for school. Next it was onto the chores: dusting, cleaning, washing, making beds and ironing. Since most houses still didn't have fridges, shopping was a daily task. As supermarkets were a rarity, this required visits to several shops: the butcher, the baker, the greengrocer and mainly on Fridays the fishmonger. The only thing that was delivered to the house in those days was milk. If she found time in the middle of the day, the 60s housewife might have a nice cup of tea with a neighbour. It was then time to collect the children from school and feed them. After that, she would prepare a supper for her husband, which they would eat together. Then it would be time to put the children to bed, reminding them to brush their teeth

The daily chores of a 1960s housewife

and wash their faces. Although it was a man's world, most fathers saw little of their children except at weekends. Women did gain employment but, with some exceptions, this was mainly outside the demands of childcare. Schools reflected this. Girls would learn what were known then as domestic sciences: cooking, sewing and household management. After leaving school, some women trained for secretarial roles; the role of school secretary being highly prized as it allowed holidays to coincide with their children's. The 1960s were a time of rapid social and economic change and by the end of the decade attitudes had changed, even though legislation trailed behind.

Typing was the mainstay of clerical work

Farming

A typical post-war tractor with open cab | Factory farming under the spotlight | Whisky maturing in white oak casks

Although the farm of the 1960s looked very different from the farm of today, increased mechanisation meant that they also looked markedly different from the pre-war farm. Fields were smaller and more work had to be done by hand than today. However by the end of the decade the greater reliance on machinery, not only shaped the crops that were grown, potatoes in particular leant themselves to machine sowing and harvesting, it also saw a 40% decline in the number of farmworkers. Even though the government had brought in controls on pesticides a decade earlier, there was a heavy reliance on chemicals both as pesticides and fertilisers. This was to have serious health implications, not only for farmworkers, but also for the general population. Farms were also dangerous places to work and the tractor, as well as being the most iconic piece of farm machinery, was also the most deadly. An annual average of 43 people were killed from 1957 to 1967 as a result of tractors overturning. This represented over one-third of work-related fatalities in agriculture. It was not until 1967 that legislation was introduced requiring all new tractors to be fitted with safety cabs.

In 1964 Ruth Harrison wrote *Animal Machines*, a seminal work in the field of meat production. The book exposed the suffering inflicted on farm animals by industrialised agriculture and led to the British government setting up a committee chaired by Francis Brambell to investigate the welfare of farm animals. The 'Brambell Report' was published in 1965 and it laid down five freedoms of animal husbandry. Namely, freedom from hunger or thirst, freedom from discomfort, freedom from pain, injury or disease, freedom to express (most) normal behaviour and freedom from fear and distress. Stanley Baker, the agricultural correspondent of the Guardian, countered Harrison's arguments when on 29th December 1964 he wrote: "Factory farming, whether we like it or not, has come to stay. The tide will not be held back, either by the humanitarian outcry of well meaning but sometimes misguided animal lovers, by the threat implicit to traditional farming methods, or by the sentimental approach to a rural way of life."

In Scotland, new strains of barley were being developed at the expense of oats and turnips. Although barley has many uses such as making malted drinks and adding to soups, it was chiefly grown for one thing, the Whisky industry.* Fuelled by rising demand from overseas markets such as America and Japan, the 1960s were boom years for Scottish distillers.

There has been much debate between whisky connoisseurs, with many claiming that scotch was a much better drink before the 1960s. While this is of course a matter of personal taste, there is no doubt that the rapid expansion of the industry and the way whisky was produced changed the tipple forever.

The Primary School

In the 1960s there were no state pre-schools or nurseries, so for most children just turning 5 years old, their first day at school was the first time they had been on their own away from home. Many mothers did not work outside the home, so this was also the first time they had been away from the home environment. Consequently, the first day of school was often a very tearful event for both child and parent. Having got over the first pangs of separation, school life soon fell into a predictable routine of learning the times tables, handwriting skills and reading out loud. School milk was part of this routine, and in the summer months it could

An older class busy painting pictures

Harvest festival celebrations

easily turn sour. In post-war Britain, a third of a pint of milk per child, was introduced in schools to supplement the child's diet. In 1971, school milk for the over-sevens was withdrawn by Margaret Thatcher, then Secretary of State for Education. For this she was dubbed 'Thatcher, Thatcher, Milk Snatcher' in the popular press. During the harsh winter of 1962-3, or the big freeze of 1963 as it became known, it was a common sight to see the small crates of milk outside the school gates with the shiny bottle tops standing proud above the bottles on a column of frozen milk. Of course the only way to defrost the school milk was to place it by the radiator, and then the poor children were forced to consume watery, lukewarm milk. And forced they were: "milk is good for your child, you WILL drink it all up!" The School Broadcasting Council for the United Kingdom had been set up in 1947 and the wireless or radio played a great part in the education of school children in the 1960s. *Music and Movement* was one such programme. All over the country in school halls, children could be found leaping and stretching to the commands on the radio. 'Now children we are going to sway like trees in the wind' would be the instruction on the radio, so all the children would begin to sway with their arms in the air. There was no 'gym kit' in primary schools so the children just removed their outer clothes and did physical education in their vests, knickers or underpants and bare feet or pumps (usually purchased from F.W. Woolworth). Visits from the school nurse would break up the daily routine. The nit nurse used to make regular visits to check for head lice.

All the children in each class would line up to be examined in turn, their hair being combed carefully with a nit comb to see if there was any infestation. There were also routine eye and hearing tests, and visits from the school dentist. Class sizes in the early 1960s were large, often over 30 children to a class, as these were the 'baby boomers', children born after the Second World War. There were no classroom assistants, just the class teacher and discipline was strict. It was quite common for a disruptive child to be rapped over the knuckles, on the buttocks or on the palm of the hand with a ruler.

A Christmas party at a school in Wales

Background

After the Second World War, the state funded secondary education system was divided using a Tripartite system containing grammar schools, secondary technical colleges and secondary modern schools. The Eleven-plus examination was used to select which pupils went to which schools based on ability. As technical colleges were not available on the scale envisaged, the exam came to symbolise fierce competition for places at the prestigious grammar schools. The very name still deeply divides opinion with many believing it was the symbol of a segregated two-tier school system whilst for others it set the educational benchmark.

Here's your chance to test yourself with example questions from the 1960s:
(Answers on page 92)

Arithmetic Questions

Question One: A train leaves London at 10:30am and arrives at Birmingham at 12:40pm. It stopped from 12:10pm to 12:20pm at Coventry which is 100 miles from London. It travelled both parts of the journey at the same rate. Find the distance from London to Birmingham.

Question Two: If 1st December falls on a Monday, on what day will Christmas Day fall that year?

Question Three: A machine makes toy soldiers at the rate of 75 in 5 minutes. How long with it take to make 6,000 of them? (answer in hours and minutes)

Question Four: Write in figures the sum of four hundred and forty six and seventy-seven.

Question Five: John is 12 years old and his mother is 42. Answer the following:

A) How old was John's mother when she was 4 times as old as him?

B) In how many years' time will his mother be three times as old as John?

C) How old will John be when his mother is 10 times as old as he was 6 years ago?

General English Questions

Question One: Change all necessary words to make these sentences plural:

A) My dog is carrying a stick.

B) His butcher has no meat.

C) A man who likes football is sure to have a team scarf in his house.

Question Two: Fill in the blank with a suitable missing word:

A) As *toe* is to *foot* so is .... to *hand*.

B) As *referee* is to *football* so is .... to *tennis*

C) As *Spain* is to .... so is *France* to *Frenchmen*

Question Three: Rewrite each of these sentences replacing the underlined words with a single word:

A) I was <u>in no doubt</u> that the shop would be closed.

B) He said that he would be coming home <u>in a short time</u>.

C) She <u>made up her mind</u> to go the cinema.

Top 10 Girls' Baby Names [1]

1. Susan — of Hebrew origin meaning "Lily Rose"
2. Julie — of French/Latin origin meaning "Youthful"
3. Karen — of Danish origin possibly via Ancient Greek Katharos meaning "Pure"
4. Jaqueline — from Hebrew via French meaning "may God protect"
5. Deborah — derived from the Hebrew word D'vorah meaning "Bee"
6. Tracey — from French and Gaelic Irish meaning "higher" or "superior"
7. Jane — from the Hebrew meaning "God is Merciful"
8. Helen — possibly from the Greek Selene meaning "Moon"
9. Diane — from Latin via French meaning "Divine"
10. Sharon — from Hebrew meaning "of the fertile plain"

Top 10 Boys' Baby Names [2]

1. David — corruption of the Hebrew name *Dawid* meaning "beloved"
2. Paul — from Latin meaning "Small" or "Humble"
3. Andrew — of Greek origin meaning "Garland or crown"
4. Mark — from the Latin name Mart-kos "consecrated to the god Mars"
5. John — of Hebrew origin meaning "God is Gracious"
6. Michael — of Hebrew origin meaning "One who is like God"
7. Stephen — of origin meaning "garland or crown"
8. Ian — a variation of John meaning "God is Gracious"
9. Robert — from the Old German meaning "Fame Bright"
10. Richard — from Old German meaning "Powerful leader"

[1,2] Data compiled by the Office for National Statistics 1954

Games, Toys and Pastimes

First manufactured in the US in 1964, the toy Rock 'Em Sock 'Em Robots that featured two robots, Red Rocker and Blue Bomber, was a basic fighting game that kept children entertained for hours on end. The aim was simple, use buttons on a pair of joysticks at the base of a platform to make the robots punch at each other. It was later marketed in the UK as Raving Bonkers. The Chatter Telephone by Fisher-Price was also popular. It first came on the market in 1962 and was a pull-along toy which worked like a dial-up telephone. Right through to the 1970s it was the company's best selling toy. In those simpler times there was also a plethora of kitchen toys such as the easy-bake oven, which taught, mostly girls, domestic science. Most children noticed that the moulded plastic pies and cakes looked the same after they came out of the oven as before they went in, so little was learnt. Card and board games were popular, seeing families gather and perhaps fall out over a game of Monopoly, Cluedo or Happy Families. Cashing in on The Beatles 'invasion' of America, Car Mascots Inc, produced a set of nodding dolls of the Fab Four. Today they are very collectable. In good condition and in their box they can fetch £2,000 at auction. The best selling boy's toy of 1964 was the Johnny Seven OMA, a multi-function toy gun made by Deluxe Reading.

Relaxing in the front room, this family has chosen some of the design trends that would come to define home furnishing in the 1960s. Despite the washed out colours in this photo, it is clear to see the bold patterns on the sitting room chairs. The clashing patterns and vivid colours that would dominate the latter half of the 1960s were already evident in 1964 as consumers with increasing disposable income aspired to make over their austere post-war home interiors.

The trend for clean lines and functional design was most obvious in the kitchen with the rise of fitted cabinetry and integrated appliances.

Record players were the mainstay of entertainment in most households. Here we see a father about to play an EP (extended play) record for his boys. EP's were a popular format in the UK until the late sixties.

With television programming for children limited to the odd programme per day, children would still spend most of their indoor time reading, drawing and playing games sat either at the dining table or on the floor in the lounge.

In the bathroom, homeowners were keen to modernise and update the layout to include fitted baths, vanity sink units and close coupled toilets. The picture above shows a woman cleaning the bath with an integrated shower attachment.

Children lucky enough to live in houses with a good sized garden would spend hours playing outdoors building dens, creating adventures and enjoying picnics. However, the park and the street were just as popular.

Design Trends in the Early Sixties

With increasing living standards and demand for modern home interiors the 1960s were a fertile time for design. British designers were making waves on the global stage as manufacturers invested in product development and aesthetic design. New materials and manufacturing techniques gave greater freedom to innovate. The trend saw sleek and streamlined furniture designs being complimented by patterned fabric textures and wall papers. With sustained economic growth during this period, British consumer confidence grew significantly as the public finally laid to rest the period of post-war shortages and austerity. This confidence was most obviously expressed in the increasing use of vivid colours in the home whether that be the carpets, the furniture or the wall coverings. Consumerism was most definitely on the rise. In the fifties, ownership of home appliances such as fridges or televisions was the preserve of the privileged few but by the early sixties it became the norm.

Whilst British design was gaining favour globally, the most influential design trends were emanating from the USA, Italy and Scandinavia. The Mid-Century Modern design movement in the USA was popular from 1945 to 1969. Its hallmarks were clean, simple lines and honest use of materials. Similar in ethos was the Scandinavian design movement which started to flourish in the 1950s. At its heart were the principles of simplicity, minimalism and functionality. Although the United Kingdom would have to wait until 1987 before seeing its first store open, the behemoth that is IKEA, founded by Ingvar Kamprad, was growing and developing in Sweden in 1962 and soon to expand to nearby Norway in 1963.

When in 1960 Elizabeth David produced her greatest work *French Provincial Cooking*, the Observer newspaper noted: "It is difficult to think that any home can do without it." By 1964, it had found its way onto the bookshelves of many homes around the country. By following her recipes British home cooks had embraced flavour and rescued culinary tastes from the bland Victorian fare prescribed by Mrs Beeton, whose recipes included an instruction to cook pasta for one and a half hours. David's path to domestic goddess status was an unorthodox one. She was born into an upper class family and came out as a debutante in 1932, but none of the men she met at various balls appealed to her. She then tried her hand at art and acting, both without much enthusiasm. It was while appearing with fellow actress Anna Neagle, that Neagle noted the young David did not even know how to make a cup of tea. When David's family suspected her of having an affair with a married man, they packed her off to the continent. It was there that she not only embraced the culture, but immersed herself in the cuisine. The resultant cookery books and humorous journals would change British tastes forever.

A Classic Gratin Dauphinois Recipe (Serves 6)

Ingredients

- 2 lbs Desiree Potatoes (which had been bred in the Netherlands in 1962. However, King Edwards will do)
- 10 fl oz full fat milk
- 10 fl oz double cream
- 2 oz butter
- 1 garlic clove, peeled and halved
- 2 sprigs of fresh thyme, plus extra for sprinkling
- 1 shallot, roughly chopped (although a small onion would do)
- A pinch of finely grated nutmeg
- 1 oz freshly grated Parmesan (a hard British cheese could also be used)
- Salt and pepper to taste

Method: Preheat the oven to Gas mark 4/ 160 degrees. Rub the butter all over the inside of a large shallow dish (about 18 by 11 inches). Peel and thinly slice the potatoes (approx 1/8" thick). Lay the slices on a tea towel and pat them dry. Keep them covered while preparing the rest of the ingredients. Pour the milk and cream into a saucepan. Add the garlic, thyme and shallot. Slowly warm the milk until just before it boils and then remove from the heat. Strain the liquid into a large jug and sprinkle with nutmeg. Layer about half the potatoes in the dish and season. Pour over half the milk and cream. Repeat with the remaining ingredients. Scatter the cheese over the top and bake for around an hour, when the potatoes should be tender and the topping golden brown. Leave to stand for 5 minutes and sprinkle over the remaining thyme. Bon appetit.

In the mid-1960s pudding made up a substantial part of most meals, be it at school or in the home. Some were fulsomely enjoyed and have stayed firm favourites, whilst others have not. Although the food producer Ambrosia had resumed production of both tinned rice and tinned macaroni puddings after the war, it was more common for them to be home-made. Other favourite puddings included jam roly-poly, chocolate sponge with chocolate sauce, apple crumble, bread and butter pudding and blancmange. Acquired tastes included sago and tapioca puddings. There was also the pudding that made schoolboys giggle, Spotted Dick, which was also known as spotted dog or railway cake, which avoided double entendres.

Spotted Dick Recipe (Serves 8)

Ingredients

- 10 oz self-raising flour
- 5 oz shredded suet
- 6 oz currants
- 4 oz caster sugar
- 2 oz mixed dried peel
- ¼ pint of milk, plus 3 tablespoons
- A pinch of salt

Method: Put the flour and salt into a mixing bowl. Add the suet, currants, sugar and mixed peel. Pour in the milk and mix to a firm but moist dough, adding extra milk if necessary. Shape into a fat roll about 8 inches long and wrap loosely in baking parchment, tying both ends with string, This will allow the pudding to rise. Place a steamer over a large pan of boiling water, add the wrapped pudding to the steamer and cook for 1½ hours. Check periodically whether the saucepan has run dry. Top up with water if necessary. Remove the pudding from the steamer and allow to cool slightly before unwrapping. Serve with custard.

Summer Holidays in 1964

In 1964 there were more choices on where to spend your hard-earned cash on a once-a-year holiday than ever before. At the top end was the growing cruise ship market. Choices included the recently launched SS Canberra. At 45,000 tons it was the largest vessel to pass through the Panama Canal to date. Competing at the luxury end of the market was the SS France, replete with two on-board swimming pools. European sun-soaked holidays were beginning to take off. In 1957 British European

The SS Canberra was an ocean liner in the P&O fleet

Airways (BEA) had introduced a route to Alicante in Eastern Spain. The term Costa Blanca was created to promote it. However, a ferry was still a more affordable way to travel with popular destinations including France, Belgium, Holland and Ireland. However, most people still holidayed at home. There were many options: the holiday camps (Warner, Butlin's or Pontins), an independently run caravan park, a bed and breakfast by the sea or simply staying with a relative by the coast. For some people all the fun of the fair came to them, be it in the form of the Highland Games in Scotland, the Grasmere Games in the Lake District or the Eisteddfod in Wales. Another popular event that draws travellers from all over the UK and beyond is the Edinburgh

The swimming pool at Butlin's Pwllheli

Fringe Festival. Starting as an unofficial adjunct to the Edinburgh International Festival in 1947, the name 'Fringe' was first coined a year later. In 1964, the Oxford Theatre Group presented the Oxford Revue which featured Monty Python founders Michael Palin and Terry Jones.

Enjoying the Eisteddfod festival in Wales

A family camping trip was a popular summer holiday choice

Radio Butlin was an integral part of the Butlin's camp experience, as immortalised in the TV sitcom Hi-De-Hi.

Campers were assigned into 'Houses' for all the sports, games and competitions. Rivalry was friendly but intense!

The Ladies Dancing competition was judged with points for the winner going towards their House total.

The inter-house Tug of War competition was particularly competitive. It drew big crowds cheering the teams on.

Children's entertainer, Uncle Boko, is pictured here presenting the "Father and Son" competition.

Redcoats would be assigned to tables to eat with campers to continue the Butlin's experience through mealtimes.

The houndstooth coat was a popular fashion item in 1964. The tessellated pattern of broken checks was most commonly black and white but other colour combinations were available, including dark red/white.

The de Haart sisters wearing designer 'Biba' coats whilst feeding the pigeons in Trafalgar Square.

At a youth fashion show, the model is wearing a polo neck and checkered trousers. Note the fashionable hairstyles in the room!

This yoke-top shift dress, complete with matching jacket, has a naval feel.

Christmas 1964

In some ways the Christmases of the mid-1960's were very similar to that of today. Families gathered together and shared much laughter and fun. But whereas today the celebrations often centre around lavish presents and the use of social media, then the celebrations were more home-made. Greeting cards would be sent to all members of the family, often the only written communication of the year. Some would contain news of the past year including news of how well the children were doing at school or in sports. In 1964, the telephone bore a greater resemblance to a table lamp than the devices of today. Calls were brief with salutations and felicitations being exchanged, all the time keeping an eye on the cost. The days of post-war rationing were still all too recent memories, so Christmas had a more frugal feel compared to today. Decorations were simple and improvised.

Tucking in to Christmas treats

Visiting Santa at his grotto

Brightly coloured paper chains were made by the family and strung across the walls in the living room. If money was tight, these could be made from strips of wallpaper. Children's TV programme Blue Peter was at hand to show you how to make your own decorations. Many of these defied health and safety standards, including how to make an advent crown from wire coat hangers, with a lit candle at each end! Food preparation began weeks, if not months, in advance. The fruit for the pudding would be steeped in alcohol, and when ready would be stirred into the batter along with a silver sixpence for luck. Few people had home freezers, so all the components of the Christmas lunch had to be purchased as close as possible to the big day. Members of the family were sent out to all four corners of the town or village to collect orders from the butcher, greengrocer and the baker as supermarkets were in their infancy. On Christmas Eve, parents would prepare a feast of mince pies and sherry (whisky in Scotland) for Father Christmas, which would disappear by morning. Sometimes a carrot would also be left for Rudolph. Children left stockings or pillow cases by their beds ready to be filled with gifts, but only if they had been good, of course! Main presents were opened after breakfast: for children these might be a watch (perhaps a Tic-a-Tic-a-Timex), Scalextric or a Sindy doll. Other favourite gifts included Etch-a-Sketch, Meccano, 3D View Master and the Amazing Magic Robot that answered questions. Relatives might also bring home made gifts, such as hand knitted jumpers and scarves. As there were no shops open on Christmas Day, the words "batteries not included" led to an occasional tearful afternoon as shops would not reopen until after Boxing Day. The day itself was one of indulgence. Very often a full English breakfast was served in the morning. The dinner itself was not always turkey as, often, the meat of choice might be chicken or goose. The best tablecloth, china, glasses and silverware were brought out for this most special of occasions, before being packed away for another year.

A festive family portrait around the tree

Overview of Radio Broadcasting

The biggest event in British radio in the early 1960s was one that could not be heard by the public, but would eventually change the way we listened to radio forever. In June 1962, the Pilkington Committee on Broadcasting published a report that would devolve BBC radio to the regions. Fearful of the impending creation of local commercial radio, the nation's broadcaster hoped to get a head start. Test closed-circuit broadcasts ran through to 1967 when BBC Radio Leicester launched. In the meantime the British public had to make do with three services, little changed since around the time of the Second World War. The Home Service, which evolved from the pre-war National Programme, featured news, entertainment and magazine programmes such as *Woman's Hour*. This was to become Radio 4. The Light Programme, launched in 1945, featured jazz and easy listening music as well as sport and light entertainment.

Broadcasting House in London

This was to become Radio 2. The Third Programme was the most highbrow of the three, playing classical music, this eventually became Radio 3. There was much to inform and entertain the listener and many have endured to this day. *Farming Today*, *The Archers*, *Any Questions?* and *In Touch* can still be heard. Other programmes seemed tired and staid and were soon to run their course. *Music While you Work*, *Housewife's Choice* and *The Dales* spoke more to an older generation than the baby boomers of the day. The last named programme, *The Dales*, had changed its name from *Mrs Dale's Diary* in 1962 and the linking narratives by Mrs Dale were dropped. This was in no small part due to the erratic behaviour of the star Ellis Powell, who struggled with alcohol addiction. On 19th February 1963, she was sacked and three months later died aged 57. The *Killing of Sister George*, a 1968 film starring Beryl Reid, is loosely based on her life. For pre-school children there was always *Listen With Mother*. Sport also featured prominently with *Test Match Special* bringing painterly descriptions of England cricket matches from around the globe. Silky voiced poet and cricket-lover John Arlott was the greatest of the commentators. The BBC was also keen on

Letter from America with Alistair Cooke

real life outside broadcasts; *Down Your Way*, a programme that toured the towns and villages of the UK, was hugely popular. What was sorely lacking in the Corporation's output was programming aimed at the youth market. There were two shows, *Pick of the Pops* and *Easy Beat*, which catered for the young, but very little else. In America, newscaster Don Gardiner interrupted the Doris Day song *Hooray for Hollywood* to announce that shots had been fired at the motorcade of President JFK. This was the first national broadcast bulletin of the news of the shooting. One programme which bridged the Atlantic and became compulsory listening for many was Alistair Cooke's *Letter from America*. In a world far less interconnected than today's, Cooke would broadcast weekly from his adopted New York. His broadcasts ranged from idle conversations with his local barkeeper to momentous events of the day.

Clint Eastwood

A Fist Full of Dollars

Directed by Sergio Leone
Starring Clint Eastwood and Marianne Koch
Released 12th September 1964 (in Italy)

When *Per un pungo di dollari*, or *A Fistful Of Dollars*, was released in the mid-1960s, the term 'Spaghetti Western' was coined as a put down to these brazen new films that dared to recreate the Wild West in a place as far away as Italy. However, the last laugh was shared by the Italian directors, whose new method of portraying colonial America in a realistic style rather than the romanticised way that was characteristic of John Wayne and his contemporaries was a huge hit in America and around the world. The plot is simple (and mostly taken from Kurosawa's *Yojimbo* of 1961). Clint Eastwood wanders into a town where clan warfare has stripped the economy to the point where only the local undertaker makes a profit and turns the two leading families against each other. Sergio Leone's best-known trademark, his dynamic use of widescreen shots, comes to the fore here as Eastwood shares a frame with no less than four of his enemies, all of whom have plenty to say to him and vice versa. It is a film not without humour and the scene where the hero asks four gunslingers to apologise to a horse is a portent of the comedy western *Blazing Saddles*. The film spawned two sequels, equally well received, namely *For a Few Dollars More* and *The Good, the Bad and the Ugly*.

Goldfinger

Directed by Guy Hamilton
Starring Sean Connery, Honor Blackman, Gert Fröbe and Tania Mallet
Released on 17th September 1964

Goldfinger was the third Bond film and was the first blockbuster of the series, firmly establishing 007 in the public imagination. *Dr. No* and *From Russia with Love* had both been successful, but *Goldfinger* outperformed both at the Box Office and in the process laid down the guidelines for nearly every Bond film that has followed since. Bond, played by dashing Sean Connery for the third time, has to find out what the unpleasant, gold-smuggling Auric Goldfinger is up to and put a stop to it. He tracks him down first to Geneva then Kentucky in a sparkling sequence of adventures, occasionally involving bumping into Goldfinger's memorable Korean hatchet-man Oddjob; the man with the weaponised hat. The film also introduced several elements which have since become cliches of the Bond series. For the first time, Bond visits Q's workshop to pick up his equipment and gadgets including the famous Aston Martin DB5. Almost as interesting as the film is how Fleming chose to name his villains. Ernő Goldfinger was a modernist architect and Fleming objected to the demolition of cottages at 2 Willow Road, Hampstead to build what he thought was a brutalist block of flats. Similarly, Thomas Blofeld (cricket commentator Henry's father) was at Eton with Fleming. A long running feud between them inspired the character Ernst Stavro Blofeld.

A Hard Day's Night

Directed by Richard Lester
Starring The Beatles
Released on 6th July 1964

The Beatles' first classic movie is a nostalgic time capsule that manages to embody a very special age of innocence from the early 1960's, when four young men from Liverpool practically took over the world with their marvellous music and charismatic charm. Director Richard Lester is to be commended for successfully capturing all of the excitement and joyful hysteria of these times for posterity. For anyone new to The Beatles who's looking to discover what they were all about, *A Hard Day's Night* is the perfect place to start. It showcases the four at the height of their early powers, before the psychedelic experimental period began and the latter breakup took its toll. The resulting motion picture is funny, clever, delightful and of course, musical. John Lennon and Paul McCartney penned several songs specifically for the film, including *Can't Buy Me Love*. The Beatles are shown travelling from gig to gig, performing music, doing interviews, trying to outsmart legions of adoring fans and generally trying to have a good time amidst all the insanity. While the Beatles themselves were not professional actors, they hardly had to be as they were essentially just being themselves, albeit exaggerated caricatures: John the sarcastic and witty one, Paul the professional lady's man, George the quiet cynic and Ringo the lovable but mistreated clown.

Julie Andrews

Mary Poppins

Directed by Robert Stevenson
Starring Julie Andrews and Dick Van Dyke
Released on 27th August 1964

Mary Poppins remains one of Disney's most iconic movies. Based on P.L. Travers' books, a nanny with magic powers comes to work for the Banks family at the request of their children to make things right for an unhappy family. It is full of memorable songs including *Chim-Chim-Cheree*, *A Spoonful of Sugar* and *Supercalifragilisticexpialidocious*. The film was one of the earliest movies to combine real-life sequences and animation successfully, making Mary Poppins' extraordinary powers more enchanting and believable. What children wouldn't want to see a nanny gliding up and down the stairs and rearranging furniture in mid-air? Julie Andrews famously joked at the podium: "I've heard of American hospitality, but this is ridiculous!" when she received an Academy Award for *Mary Poppins*. When she won her Golden Globe, she seemed to sincerely thank Jack Warner for "making all this possible" thereby having the last laugh. Warner had blocked her involvement in the film adaptation of *My Fair Lady*, giving her the opportunity to win an Oscar for a different movie in the same year. Audrey Hepburn who played Eliza Doolittle wasn't even nominated. And then there was Dick Van Dyke's 'cockney' accent in *Mary Poppins*. He apologised for it in 2014 saying when asked what part of Britain he was from: "a little shire in the north where most of the people were from Ohio."

My Fair Lady

Audrey Hepburn

Directed by George Cukor
Starring Audrey Hepburn and Rex Harrison
Released on 21st October 1964

A professor of phonetics, Henry Higgins (Rex Harrison) wagers that he can pass cockney street urchin Eliza Doolittle (Audrey Hepburn) off as a sophisticated lady. Higgins is a confirmed misanthropic bachelor with his interest in Eliza originally purely professional. However, while she is the one who is supposed to be changing, he seems to be changing too, falling for Eliza. The star of the show is the beautiful music created by Lerner and Loewe including *I Could Have Danced All Night*, *A Little Bit of Luck*, *Wouldn't it be Loverly*, *Show Me* and *On the Street Where You Live*. However, the song *A Hymn to Him (Why Can't A Woman Be More Like a Man?)* is open to interpretation. Much has been made of the fact that Hepburn's singing was dubbed and that Harrison's 'talk-singing' jars, but the film was well received and won 8 Oscars. There is a strong supporting cast including the visiting colonel (Wilfrid Hyde-White) and Eliza's father (Stanley Holloway), who provide a pleasing distraction from the main story. The reality is that *Pygmalion*, the 1913 George Bernard Shaw play the film was based on, looked back to the Victorian era. By the time of the film's release, Doris Lessing's *The Golden Notebook* and Sylvia Plath's *The Bell Jar* had also been released and to many the story seemed dated.

The Pink Panther

Peter Sellers

Directed by Blake Edwards   Music by Henri Mancini
Starring David Niven and Peter Sellers
Released on 20th March 1964 (USA)

David Niven was given top-billing for this movie having already won an Oscar his for role in the 1958 film adaptation of Terence Rattigan's play *Separate Tables*. Although Peter Sellers was known to British audiences for his various roles in Ealing comedies and the hit radio broadcast *The Goon Show*, he was less well known overseas. But it was Sellers, in the role of the clumsy Inspector Jacques Clouseau who stole the show. In this movie, the famously clumsy and seemingly idiotic detective is searching for the Pink Panther, a diamond so named because a slight discolouration created the image of a rose-coloured feline. It has, not by chance, come into the possession of suave jewel thief Charles Litton (David Niven) and his worthless nephew George (Robert Wagner). There is a great supporting cast, with Claudia Cardinale as Princess Dala (the stone's owner) and the French model/actress Capucine as Clouseau's long-suffering wife Simone. A slight warning, however: if you're expecting to see Cato (Bert Kwouk) tackle Clouseau when the latter returns home, or if you're expecting to see Commissioner Dreyfus (Herbert Lom) rant about his hatred of Clouseau, you will be disappointed, Those characters didn't appear until the next film in the series, *A Shot in the Dark*, also released in 1964.

Bewitched

First aired 17th September 1964

Starring Elizabeth Montgomery, Dick York and Agnes Moorehead

Bewitched, a beloved American television sitcom that premiered in 1964, enchanted audiences with its magical blend of fantasy and humour. The show, created by Sol Saks, revolves around Samantha Stephens, played by Elizabeth Montgomery. She is a charming suburban housewife who happens to be a witch married to a mortal man named Darrin Stephens, portrayed by Dick York in the early seasons. The series captivated viewers with Samantha's attempts to balance her supernatural abilities with the challenges of suburban life and her husband's disapproval of using magic. The central conflict often arose from Darrin's desire for a normal, magic-free life, leading to comedic situations and misunderstandings. Agnes Moorehead portrayed Samantha's witty and mischievous mother, Endora, adding an extra layer of magic and humour. *Bewitched* ran for eight successful seasons until 1972, leaving an enduring legacy in the realm of classic television. The show's innovative premise, combined with the chemistry of its talented cast, made it a timeless favourite, influencing subsequent generations of sitcoms. The magic of *Bewitched* lies not only in its supernatural elements but also in its ability to weave enchanting narratives around the universal themes of love, family and acceptance. It also left every child wishing that they to could cast a spell by cutely wiggling their nose. After the series ended Montgomery, for fear of being typecast, accepted mainly hard-hitting roles, including that of alleged axe-murderer Lizzie Borden.

Noele Gordon

Crossroads

First aired 2nd November 1964

Starring Noele Gordon, Jane Rossington and Roger Tonge

Crossroads was created by Lew Grade's ATV company and was only scheduled to run for 13 weeks. It began life as a late afternoon series (we didn't call them soap operas in the sixties) set in the fictional King's Oak Crossroads Motel, somewhere in the West Midlands. The series originally centred around the character of the flame-haired widow Meg Richardson, the Motel owner (played by Noele Gordon). The other main characters were Meg's daughter Jill and son Sandy, their cousin Brian Jarvis, Meg's sister Kitty Jarvis and her husband Dick, the motel's Spanish chef Carlos, waitress Marilyn Gates and receptionist Diane Lawton. The immortal first words were "Crossroads Motel. Can I help you?". Probably the best-loved of all *Crossroads* characters though, was the slow-witted, woolly-hatted Benny Hawkins, first seen as a labourer at Diane's uncle's farm. Benny had an infatuation with "Miss Diane" and was central to one of the funniest plot holes in television history when he went out for a spanner and returned nine months later. The series was also infamous for its wonky sets and actors forgetting their lines. The character most famous for the latter was Amy Turtle (Ann George) who was immortalised as Mrs Overall, played by Julie Walters in Victoria Wood's parody *Acorn Antiques*. Towards the end of the series the motel burnt down and viewers assumed that Meg had gone up in flames with it, but she'd actually booked a luxury berth on the QE2 to start a new life 'down under'.

Peyton Place

First aired 15th September 1964

Starring Dorothy Malone, Mia Farrow, Ed Nelson and Ryan O'Neal

Ryan O'Neal

Based on Grace Metalious's steamy best-selling novel, this romantic and tempestuous drama was set in the small New England town of Peyton Place, a community seething with extramarital affairs and dark secrets of every kind. It was the first major American soap, and also the first to be screened on British television. The saga told of the lives and loves of the Harringtons, Carsons, Mackenzies and Andersons. With complicated love affairs with breathless sex, every episode ended with a cliff-hanger. One plot line was the pregnancy, miscarriage and loveless marriage of Betty Anderson (Barbara Parkins) to rich Rodney Harrington (Ryan O'Neal) who really loved the chaste Allison. Another story line was the love of full-time bookshop-owner and part-time emotional wreck Constance Mackenzie (Dorothy Malone) for Rossi, the only man who knew that Elliot Carson, the father of Constance's illegitimate daughter Allison (Mia Farrow), was serving 18 years in prison. As the show went on Betty, stunning but certifiable, married Steven Cord who had defended Rodney on a murder charge, then two years later remarried Rodney. In the face of dwindling ratings *Peyton Place* came to an end with Dr. Rossi arrested for murder and Rodney in a wheelchair. In 1977, this and other American soap operas were brilliantly parodied by the US series *Soap*, which nearly didn't make it to our screens as studio chiefs objected to its emphasis on sex and infidelity. Had they not seen *Peyton Place*?

Play School

First broadcast on 21st April 1964

Featuring numerous presenters including Brian Cant and Derek Griffiths

Play School, which ran from 1964 to 1987, left an indelible mark on the shape of children's television in the UK. It was shown five mornings a week on BBC Two, and eventually repeated at the start of the afternoon's BBC One children's schedule. It was aimed at pre-school children and its format remained almost unchanged featuring songs, dances, dressing up and pets and of course the famous windows. Before Microsoft was even thought of, *Play School's* windows opened up a whole world of film sequences including factory visits, the countryside and other stuff. There were famously three windows, square, round and arched and children would sit entranced, wondering which one would be chosen. There was apparently a clue to the kind of film that followed, depending on the shape of window, but that level of subtlety was probably lost on the average four-year-old. There were of course the dolls: Humpty, Jemima, Big and Little Ted and Hamble, who was replaced by Poppy in the mid-1980s. Like the line-up of a manufactured pop group, there was something for everyone in this unforgettable combo. In 1971 a spin-off, *Play Away*, was made. Aimed at older children, it was less educational and more fun based. Brian Cant was on hand to leave no stone unturned in search of a pun-based joke and Derek Griffiths popped up, guitar in hand, to provide musical entertainment. The show was famous for early appearances of people who went on to bigger things like Jeremy Irons, Anita Dobson and Tony Robinson.

Seven Up!
First aired 5th May 1964
Directed by Paul Almond

The programme selected 14 children, all aged seven, from a variety of contrasting class, gender and ethnic backgrounds, and then asked them a series of questions about who they were, what they liked, what they thought of the world around them and most significantly, what they thought would happen to them in the future. Of the 14 children, roughly six were 'working class' or poor, four were 'upper class' and four were notionally 'middle class'. Only four were female; only one was black. *Seven Up!* adopted a very straightforward question and answer format, quizzing each child in their respective learning environment, then throwing them all together to watch the bemused collision of class and etiquette on a visit to London Zoo, at a party and in an adventure playground. In doing so, the *World in Action* production team created a piece of television which, unknowingly, provided the root for the development of the most ambitious, significant and influential television documentary project ever. Unbelievably in retrospect, the original film was perceived as a one-off with no thought given to checking to see if any of the 14 kids actually did realise their dreams by the year 2000. But at the end of the 1960s, producer Michael Apted proposed to Granada another one-off film returning to see how each of the children was progressing, which was shown as *7 plus Seven* in 1970. The programme was then produced at seven year intervals. The last programme, *63 up*, was produced in 2019.

Top of the Pops
First aired on 1st January 1964
Created by Johnnie Stewart and Stanley Dorfman

The BBC marked the New Year with a new show aimed at a younger audience than it had previously catered for. The first episode was broadcast live from a converted church in Dickenson Road, Rusholme, Manchester. Dusty Springfield *(I Only want to Be With You)* was the first artist to sing on the show. Other guests included The Rolling Stones, The Dave Clark Five and The Hollies. Originally the show had a set resembling a coffee bar disco and the DJ's sat at turntables. Around 150 local youngsters were brought in each week to dance and mill around the stages. Denise Sampey spun the records for the first few programmes before being replaced by model Samantha Juste. In 1967, Juste left for California to be with her husband Mickey Dolenz of The Monkees. The format of *Top of the Pops* was simple and changed little; a few coloured lights, some camera effects (not always state-of-the-art), and an artist, usually lip-syncing, not always successfully. From the start, there was no pretence that the music was actually being played live. In 1967, Jimi Hendrix was seen attempting to mime to *Purple Haze* while an Alan Price record was being inadvertently played in the background. Cliff Richard and Status Quo both appeared in four different decades, while Tom Jones holds the record for the longest gap between performances for the same song when he sang *It's Not Unusual* in February 1965 and again in June 1987.

Entertaining Mr. Sloane

Written by Joe Orton

Premiered 6th May 1964 at the New Arts Theatre, London

Entertaining Mr. Sloane, a dark comedy, marked a significant moment in British theatre. The play is a subversive and provocative exploration of sexual manipulation, generational conflict and the hypocrisy of moral standards. Set in a bland London suburb, the plot revolves around the enigmatic Mr. Sloane, a sly, attractive young man who becomes a lodger in the home of Kath, a middle-aged woman living with her elderly, irascible father, Kemp. Sloane's arrival ignites a bizarre, tension-filled dynamic within the household. Kath, sexually frustrated and desperate for attention, is immediately infatuated with Sloane, while her brother, Ed, a closeted, authoritative figure, also becomes enamoured with him, offering him a job and protection. The play unfolds as a game of seduction and power. Sloane manipulates both siblings to secure his position, leveraging their sexual desires against each other. The characters represent broader societal themes; Kath and Ed embody the disillusionment and moral bankruptcy of the middle class, while Kemp, who recognises Sloane as a figure from his dark past, represents the neglected and powerless elderly. Orton's writing is characterised by sharp, witty dialogue and a flair for the absurd. He exposes the veneer of respectability and challenges social norms, particularly those relating to sexuality and authority.

Zero Mostel in the title role

Fiddler on the Roof

Music by Jerry Rick and Lyrics by Sheldon Harnick

Opened on Broadway on 22nd September 1964

The story, set in the Pale of Settlement of Imperial Russia in 1905, is based on *Tevye and his Daughters* (and other tales) by Sholem Aleichem. The central character of the musical is Tevye, a milkman in the small village of Anatevka, who is trying to maintain his Jewish religious and cultural traditions as outside influences encroach upon the lives of the community's residents. He must cope with the strong-willed actions of his three older daughters, who wish to marry for love, Each one's choice of a husband moves further away from the customs of their Jewish faith and heritage. This causes Tevye to question the roles of tradition in a changing world. Key songs from the show include *Tradition*, *If I Were a Rich Man* and *Sunrise, Sunset*. The title of the musical comes from a painting by Marc Chagall, *The Fiddler*, which inspired the idea of a fiddler on the roof representing tradition, yet precariously balancing on the edge of change. The musical was groundbreaking for its time, with its serious musical exploration of themes such as religion, tradition and persecution set against the backdrop of the Russian pogroms against Jews. It won nine Tony Awards, including Best Musical, Score, Book, Direction and Choreography. The original Broadway production of the show became the first musical in history to surpass 3,000 performances.

House of the Rising Sun

Performed by The Animals   Arranged by Alan Price

Released: 19th June 1964

The Animals

There are many theories about the identity of The House of The Rising Sun, the best guess is that was a brothel in New Orleans. It was named after its proprietor Madame Marianne LeSoleil Levant (which means 'Rising Sun' in French) and was open for business from 1862 until 1874. The song's melody is a traditional English ballad, but it became popular as an African-American folk song. It had been recorded by Texas Alexander in the 1920s, then by a number of other artists including Leadbelly, Woody Guthrie, Josh White and later Nina Simone. It was her version The Animals first heard. No one can claim rights to the song, meaning it can be recorded and sold royalty-free. The Animals recorded it in one take, as they had perfected the song from performing it on the road. The band drove to London from Liverpool on May 17th 1964 and recorded what would become their most iconic number.

Oh, Pretty Woman

Performed by Roy Orbison   Written by Roy Orbison and Bill Dees

Released: 15th August 1964

Roy Orbison

Roy Orbison was writing with his songwriting partner Bill Dees at his house when he told Dees to get start playing anything that came to mind. Orbison's wife Claudette came in and said she was going to go into town to buy something. Orbison asked if she needed any money and Dees joked: "Pretty woman never needs any money." Inspired, Orbison started singing, "Pretty woman walking down the street." Dees stated in a later interview: "He sang it while I was banging my hand down on the table and by the time she returned we had the song. I love the song. From the moment that the rhythm started, I could hear the heels clicking on the pavement, click, click, the pretty woman walking down the street, in a yellow skirt and red shoes. We wrote *Oh, Pretty Woman* on a Friday, the next Friday we recorded it and the next Friday it was out."

A Hard Day's Night

Written and performed by The Beatles   Released: 10th July 1964

The Beatles

The title was taken from an expression Ringo used. In a 1964 interview with DJ Dave Hull, Ringo explained: "We went to do a job, and we'd worked all day and we happened to work all night. I came up still thinking it was day I suppose, and I said, 'It's been a hard day...' and I looked around and saw it was dark, so I said, 'Night!' So we came to *A Hard Day's Night*." John Lennon wrote this song, which contains long, repeating notes that are uncommon in pop music. Even more unusual, Lennon sang it in glissando: "haaaard days night...". The melody resembles the Irish folk song *Donall Og*, with the same pentatonic and small glissandos. You can even find such glissandos in the English ballad *Three Babes*. Albert Goldman wrote in his 1980 book *The Lives of John Lennon*: "The whole composition is written in mixolydic key, an old key which was abandoned in the beginning of the seventeenth century but is maintained in English and Irish folk music." This was also the title song to the first of five Beatles movies.

The Kinks

All Day and All of the Night
Performed by The Kinks   Written by Ray Davies
Released: 23rd October 1964

The Kinks based this song on their first hit, *You Really Got Me*. In their early years, The Kinks' record company pressured them to follow up hits very quickly, which created what lead singer Ray Davies described as an "assembly line" of songs. In this case, the tactic worked well with the sound-a-like tune scoring them another hit. Kinks frontman Ray Davies wrote this lusty rocker where the guy can't stand to be away from his girl even for a minute. He called it: "A neurotic song; youthful, obsessive and sexually possessive." There was a persistent rumour that Jimmy Page played guitar on some early Kinks songs, including this one. When Ray Davies was asked about this in a 1981 interview he replied: "I remember Page coming to one of our sessions when we were recording. Page came in to hear Dave's solo and he laughed. And now he says that he played it! So I think he's an asshole, and he can put all the curses he wants on me because I know I'm right and he's wrong."

Dionne Warwick

Walk On By
Performed by Dionne Warwick   Written by Burt Bacharach and Hal David
Released: 26th April 1964

This could easily be an answer to The Kinks possessive song *All Day and All of the Night*, but it was written earlier. The songwriting team of Burt Bacharach and Hal David wrote this song. Bacharach came up with the music and David wrote the lyrics about a woman asking her former lover to leave her alone. This was released as the B-side to Warwick's single *Any Old Time Of The Day*. She had several releases that went nowhere and her latest tune was, in the opinion of her label, her manager and herself, her last shot at making the Top 40. Murray the K, whose show on radio station WINS was the top-rated program in New York, wouldn't play it. No matter how many people called and pleaded with him, he played the B-side instead because he knew that was the tune with potential. Warwick's record company wasn't happy with this, but listeners agreed with Murray and *Walk On By* became a massive hit.

Cilla Black

You're My World
Performed by Cilla Black   Written by Umberto Bindi, Gino Paoli, Carl Sigman
Released: May 6th 1964

Cilla Black was discovered by Beatles manager Brian Epstein. She went on to become the most successful female singer of the Mersey boom. Later she became a leading TV presenter in Britain, hosting the successful BBC music show *Cilla* between 1968 and 1976 and in the 1980s and 1990s mainstream ITV hits *Blind Date* and *Surprise Surprise*. After topping the UK charts with a cover of Dionne Warwick's *Anyone Who Had a Heart*, former Cavern Club coat-check girl Cilla Black was given this booming song as a follow up. Produced by George Martin, it was originally an Italian ballad called *Il Mio Mondo*, which he had translated by Carl Sigman and arranged by Johnny Pearson, becoming *You're My World*. It went on to become her second UK Number 1 and sold worldwide including in the United States where it became her only hit.

The Shangri-Las

Leader of the Pack

Performed by the Shangri-Las   Written by Morton, Barry and Greenwich

Released: 20th September 1964

This is the ultimate karaoke song. All you need is a good lead vocalist, some backing singers and someone who cannot sing to do the motorcycle noises. The leader of the pack is the archetypical bad boy; the guy you definitely don't want your daughter to date. He's head of a motorcycle gang, and in this song, the girl falls for him big time. Her father forbids her from seeing him, so she breaks it off. 'The Leader' gives her one last kiss, then rides off into the rain, meeting his doom when he crashes his bike. "The leader of the pack, and now he's gone, gone, gone, gone, gone, gone". *Leader of the Pack* was banned from radio and television in the UK because of trouble between mods and rockers. Lead vocalist, Mary Weiss, later landed in Britain wearing a leather jacket to show everyone what side she was on. As the saying goes "no publicity is bad publicity."

Petula Clark

Downtown

Performed by Petula Clark   Written by Tony Hatch

Recorded 16th October 1964

This was Petula Clark's first hit in the US, which was slow to discover her talents. In the UK, she was a star as a singer and as a television performer where she was a regular on the BBC. In the early '60s, she also caught on in France when she started recording her songs in French. Oddly, she didn't get an American record deal until late in 1964 when a Warner Bros. executive named Joe Smith, who was holidaying in England, heard the song and signed her to a deal. When *Downtown* was released in the US, it shot to #1 making Petula the first female singer from the UK to hit #1 in the US during the rock era (post 1955). Remarkably, she didn't even promote the song before it hit the top spot, as she was touring French-speaking countries at the time.

Lulu

Shout

Performed by Lulu and The Luvvers   Written by The Isley Brothers

Peaked in the charts on 24th June 1964

The Isley Brothers wrote this on the spur of the moment at a Washington, DC concert in mid-1959. As they performed Jackie Wilson's *Lonely Teardrops*. Ronald Isley ad-libbed, "WELLLLLLLLLLL... you know you make me want to SHOUT" and Rudy and O'Kelly joined in on the improvisation. The audience went wild and afterwards, RCA executive Howard Bloom suggested putting it out as their first single for the record label. In the UK, this is the song that introduced the singing sensation Lulu. The Scottish singer came to London at age 15 and recorded a version of the song with her group Lulu & The Luvvers. It made it to #7 in the UK in 1964. Early on, Lulu often performed in blues clubs where the song was a great fit. She soon became a very successful actress as well, appearing in the film *To Sir With Love* and scoring a #1 US hit with the title track.

Top of the Pops in 1964

There were 24 number one records in 1964 in the UK single charts published by the NME. The best selling single of the year was *Can't Buy Me Love* by The Beatles.

I Want to Hold Your Hand
The Beatles
From 12th Dec 1963 for 5 weeks

Glad All Over
The Dave Clark Five
From 16th Jan 1964 for 2 weeks

Needles and Pins
The Searchers
From 30th Jan 1964 for 3 weeks

Diane
The Bachelors
From 20th Feb 1964 for 1 week

Anyone Who Had a Heart
Cilla Black
From 27th Feb 1964 for 3 weeks

Little Children
Billy J. Kramer and the Dakotas
From 19th Mar 1964 for 2 weeks

Can't Buy Me Love
The Beatles
From 2nd Apr 1964 for 3 weeks

A World Without Love
Peter and Gordon
From 23rd Apr 1964 for 2 weeks

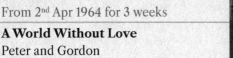

Don't Throw Your Love Away
The Searchers
From 7th May 1964 for 2 weeks

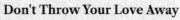

Juliet
The Four Pennies
From 21st May 1964 for 1 week

You're My World
Cilla Black
From 28th May 1964 for 4 weeks

It's Over
Roy Orbison
From 25th Jun 1964 for 2 weeks

The House of the Rising Sun
The Animals
From 9th Jul 1964 for 1 week

It's All Over Now
The Rolling Stones
From 16th Jul 1964 for 1 week

A Hard Day's Night
The Beatles
From 23rd Jul 1964 for 3 weeks

Do Wah Diddy Diddy
Manfred Mann
From 13th Aug 1964 for 2 weeks

Have I the Right?
The Honeycombs
From 27th Aug 1964 for 2 weeks

You Really Got Me
The Kinks
From 10th Sep 1964 for 2 weeks

I'm Into Something Good
Herman's Hermits
From 24th Sep 1964 for 2 weeks

Oh, Pretty Woman
Roy Orbison
8th Oct for 2 wks then 12th Nov for 1 wk

Always Something There to Remind Me
Sandie Shaw
From 22nd Oct 1964 for 3 weeks

Baby Love
The Supremes
From 19th Nov 1964 for 2 weeks

Little Red Rooster
The Rolling Stones
From 3rd Dec 1964 for 1 week

I Feel Fine
The Beatles
From 10th Dec 1964 for 5 weeks

The Beatles Conquer America and Canada

The Beatles at Kennedy airport

After touring Europe, Hong Kong and Australia, the Fab Four headed for the States and Canada to embark on a 32 concert tour. Music writer Jane Skinner Sawyers described the tour as "the first major rock-and roll concert tour in the history of popular music," in her 2006 book *Read the Beatles*. In 1964 they took North America by storm, but not everyone was impressed. Full time entomologist and part-time music critic Theodore Strongin wrote in the New York Times "The Beatles' vocal quality can be described as hoarsely incoherent, with the minimal enunciation necessary to communicate the schematic texts. Two theories were offered in at least one household to explain the Beatles' popularity." Strongin profered: "We haven't had an idol in a few years. The Beatles are different, and we have to get rid of our excess energy somehow. The other theory is that the longer parents object with such high dudgeon, the longer children will squeal so hysterically." It is ironic that during his scientific career he identified several species of rare beetles, but never quite got the Beatles craze of 1964. However, the tour did not pass without incident. Variety Magazine reported that at the concert in Vancouver, Canada, 160 girls were treated for injuries and trauma as thousands of fans charged the security barriers in front of the stage. In Cleveland and Kansas City, full scale riots were prevented when Beatles' press officer Derek Taylor threatened to cancel the concerts. Even so, despite curmudgeonly reviews and the odd disturbance, The Beatles tour of North America was a huge success. It was the first million dollar rock tour.

Meanwhile, The Rolling Stones Conquer Wiltshire

The Rolling Stones

It seems unbelievable now to imagine a time when The Rolling Stones, one of the all-time great bands, would have played even one gig in small venues in the tranquil West Country, let alone five in one year! But they did, in 1964. The band had made their live debut in Wiltshire at Salisbury's Gaumont Theatre on Sunday 27th October 1963. They played fourth on the bill to The Everly Brothers, Bo Diddley and Little Richard. They returned to the same venue the following year on Thursday 17th January 1964. It was also the first of five separate shows they played in Wiltshire that year. At this stage they had yet to release their debut album, and had so far only released two moderately successful singles, but the band were on the cusp of greatness and the reception they received this time proved their emerging popularity. The gig poster shows that admission on the night was seven shillings and sixpence, which in today's money works out at a meagre 37 pence. The very next night, The Stones played their second gig in Wiltshire at Salisbury's City Hall. They returned to the same venue on Saturday 18th March. But by now it was clear the band had outgrown playing venues at this level, as evidenced by the sheer length of the queues to see them, but they did return to play their very last gig in Wiltshire. It took place in August outside Longleat stately home in front of 16,000 fans.

The Royal Variety Performance on 2nd November 1964 at The London Palladium

in the presence of Her Majesty Queen Elizabeth II

This year's Royal Variety Performance at the Palladium was notably missing The Beatles, who were busy conquering America. However, Liverpool's own Jimmy Tarbuck stepped into the spotlight, dazzling the audience with his quick wit and affable charm. For many in attendance, it was their first introduction to this rising star, and Tarbuck later described the experience as "the greatest, most wonderful day of my life." Another Liverpudlian sensation, Cilla Black, made her Royal Variety debut, admitting to feeling nervous about the occasion. "I keep dreaming that just before I bow to the Royal Box I fall flat on my face before all those famous people!" Despite her apprehension, Black delivered a stellar performance that left both the Queen and the audience thoroughly impressed. The evening showcased a diverse array of talent, including British comedy from Morecambe and Wise and the unpredictable Tommy Cooper. Gracie Fields serenaded the crowd, while Russia's Moiseyev Dance Company wowed with their graceful movements. Juggling maestro Gil Dova, whose father had survived the Hindenburg Disaster, provided a captivating spectacle. Representing America, deadpan comedian Bob

Cilla Black

Lena Horne

Morecambe and Wise

Newhart and singer and civil rights activist Lena Horne took the stage. Horne's rendition of *Stormy Weather*, a poignant reminder of wartime struggles, struck a chord with those who had lived through World War II. Bob Newhart joined the ranks of many Royal Variety Performance artists who faced the stress of international travel delays en route to the show. His plane was diverted to West Germany, causing him to arrive at the Palladium in the midst of the run-through. Fortunately, his act did not require music, alleviating some of his anxiety. A particularly moving moment occurred when The Bachelors directed a line from one of their songs to the Queen, earning spontaneous applause from the audience. Despite some behind-the-scenes mishaps, including the mysterious disappearance and subsequent recovery of the Tiller Girls' costumes, the show went on without a hitch. Executive Producer Robert Nesbitt's innovative staging, which featured female recording stars Cilla Black, Millicent Martin, Kathy Kirby, and Brenda Lee entering on a revolving stage seated in gleaming sports cars, perfectly encapsulated the spirit of the Swinging Sixties.

The Bachelors

One of today's more eclectic labels, Nonesuch Records, was founded in 1964 as an independently-funded classical label, releasing albums of baroque music by composers like Handel. It soon ventured into presenting music from modern and contemporary composers like Stravinsky and Ives. The business philosophy was to make classical music available to listeners on a smaller budget. Also in classical music, Spanish tenor Plácido Domingo made his international breakthrough at the première of Ginastera's *Don Rodrigo* in New York City. Andy Warhol once famously said "art is anything you can get away with," borrowing the words of Canadian philosopher Marshall McLuhan. His work of 1964, *Empire*, tested this hypothesis. The film consists of just over eight hours of an

Artist Andy Warhol

unchanging view of the Empire State Building. There is no commentary or characters. Warhol stated that the true purpose of the film was "to see time go by." Another person who had a fluid attitude to art was photographer Dorothy Podber. In 1964, she entered Warhol's workshop The Factory and shot at a pile of screen prints the artist had made of Marilyn Monroe. Far from reducing their value, she increased their collectability exponentially. Also in Pop Art, Roy Lichtenstein's comic book-inspired paintings, such as *Whaam!* and *Drowning Girl*, exemplified the movement's engagement with popular media and its critique of artistic conventions. March saw the publication of Beatle John Lennon's *In His Own Write*, a compendium of nonsense verse and drawings. In poetry, the most important lines to be read were, "I was only that which, you touched with your palm over which, in the deaf, raven-black night, you bent your head...I was practically blind. You,

John Lennon

appearing, then hiding, taught me to see." But, these were not read on stage or in an academic seminar, but in a Soviet courtroom. The poet, Joseph Brodsky, was sentenced to five years hard labour for 'social parasitism'. He eventually defected to America and became Poet Laureate of The United States in 1991. March saw the death of the firebrand playwright Brendan Behan (author of *Borstal Boy* and *The Quare Fellow*) whose quote: "I am a drinker with writing problems" all too tragically summed up his short life. The world of literature also lost Edith Sitwell who once said "My personal hobbies are reading, listening to music and silence." Ian Fleming also left us having seen only two of his James Bond novels made into films, namely *Dr. No* and *From Russia With Love*. He was however on set for the filming of *Goldfinger*, but died before its release. As well as the Bond series of books his lasting legacy was one of the most magical children's books ever written, *Chitty Chitty Bang Bang*, which he wrote for his son Casper. On the stage, the musical *Fiddler on the Roof* premiered on Broadway on 22nd September. With music by Jerry Bock and lyrics by Sheldon Harnick, the musical, based on Sholem Aleichem's stories, depicted the struggles of a Jewish family in Tsarist Russia. Its success demonstrated the enduring power of musical theatre to convey complex narratives while incorporating memorable songs, such as *Tradition* and *If I Were a Rich Man*.

Author Ian Fleming

Funeral in Berlin
Author: Len Deighton   First published in 1964

In Deighton's third instalment of the *Unnamed Spy* series, *Funeral In Berlin*, the author masterfully captures the atmosphere of Cold War paranoia that gripped the world in the mid-sixties. The protagonist is tasked with facilitating the defection of Semitsa, a top Soviet scientist, but as is often the case, there are layers of intrigue beyond a simple change of allegiance. Enter Colonel Stok, a formidable antagonist orchestrating his own manoeuvres against the West. Amidst a web of deception, everyone harbours ulterior motives, gradually unveiled in the climactic chapters. Like a chess match, the story unfolds with strategic moves and counter-moves, with the hero striving to avoid becoming a mere pawn sacrificed in the larger scheme. Against the backdrop of Cold War politics, lingering shadows of the past including lost Nazi funds add layers of complexity to the narrative. It results in a riveting and thoroughly enjoyable read.

A Caribbean Mystery
Author: Agatha Christie   Published: 16th November 1964

Miss Marple, the beloved character created by Agatha Christie appears in 12 novels and 20 short stories. Residing in the quaint English village of St. Mary Mead with its cozy local pub, a scattering of shops, and the grandeur of the Gossington Hall estate. However, in this particular tale, Miss Marple finds herself whisked away to the fictional Caribbean island of St. Honoré for a much-needed respite. Her tranquil holiday takes an unexpected turn when she encounters Major Palgrave, an incessant storyteller. He regales her with a tale of murder and tantalisingly offers to reveal the identity of the culprit in a photograph. Yet, at the eleventh hour, he retreats from his offer. Despite this initial setback, a series of murders ensue thrusting Miss Marple into the role of detective as she endeavours to uncover the truth and thwart further bloodshed. *A Caribbean Mystery* is the 9th book in series with the final story, *Sleeping Murder*, being published in 1976.

Martian Time-Slip
Author: Philip K. Dick   First published in 1964

The story unfolds on Mars, yet the backdrop is anything but fantastical. Despite the relative success of colonisation efforts, life on the desolate Martian terrain remains a struggle. Humanity scrapes by with limited water supplies, grapples with malfunctioning equipment, faces exorbitant costs for Earth-bound replacements, deals with financial obligations, craves power and contends with petty disputes. Amidst these mundane trials, the central narrative emerges through the intersecting stories of a disparate cast of characters, ultimately coalescing around the theme of property speculation. *Martian Time Slip* is best experienced in written form. Notably, Stanley Kubrick declined an opportunity to adapt it into a film. However, Isa Dick Hackett, daughter of the author Philip K. Dick, successfully produced the critically acclaimed miniseries *Electric Dreams* in 2017, drawing inspiration from this work and others penned by her father.

You Only Live Twice

Author: Ian Fleming   First Published: 26th March 1964

The last James Bond novel written and edited in Ian Fleming's lifetime, *You Only Live Twice* is one of the more absorbing Bond outings. For starters it is a sequel to the events of *On Her Majesty's Secret Service*, dealing with a widowed and emotionally-shattered 007 sent to Japan on a near-impossible diplomatic mission. Featuring a characterisation of Bond not seen before, it also allows Fleming to indulge in some travelogue writing, catching from a Westerner's point of view early sixties Japan, a rising power as seen from a diminishing one. It's also, for all of the suspense and action in the final act, a surprisingly morbid book, with a borderline obsession with death and a sense of winding down clear from both its author and its main character. All of which results in some of the most meaningful and intriguing chapters in the Bond canon.

A Moveable Feast

Author: Ernest Hemingway   First published in 1964

In his posthumously published memoir, Hemingway delves into his time spent in Paris following the aftermath of World War I. The title, *A Moveable Feast*, aptly captures the essence of his experiences, akin to enjoying a banquet with a constellation of bohemian luminaries. Among them, luminaries such as Joyce, Pound, Ford Madox Ford, and Scott Fitzgerald, who all are enjoying the French capital at the same time. Hemingway also meticulously documents his culinary adventures. Food, art, alcohol, and racing form the backbone of his reminiscences. Hemingway's writing style mirrors that of his fiction: casual, affectionate, and consistently engaging. Its deceptively simple prose draws readers in. However, his memoir offers profound insights into the workings of the writer's mind and the delicate balance between creative inspiration and its elusive nature.

The Swimmer

Author: John Cheever   First Published: 18th July 1964

In a whimsical yet poignant tale, a middle-aged man embarks on an unconventional journey to swim his way home. Several miles from his destination, he utilises every available pool along his route, be they private or public, wearing only in his bathing suit. Initially, the narrative has a lighthearted tone, exploring the absurdity of his endeavour. However, as the story progresses, it takes a darker and more introspective turn as he reflects on his own life and delves into the hidden complexities of his neighbours' lives. By the time he reaches his doorstep, he finds himself confronting the depths of despair, his journey serving as a metaphorical descent into personal turmoil. Originally published in The New Yorker, this compact yet profoundly impactful story is only a mere ten pages, yet its resonance is felt far beyond its length. *The Swimmer* is widely hailed as the greatest American short story of the latter half of the 20th century.

Charlie and the Chocolate Factory
Author: Roald Dahl   Publication Date: 23rd November 1964 (UK)

Charlie Bucket and his family live a very poor existence, Charlie's one pleasure is in receiving a single bar of Wonka's chocolate on his birthday. However, excitement sweeps through the town when it's announced that the enigmatic Willy Wonka will open his legendary factory to five fortunate children for an exclusive tour. With the tantalising prospect of five golden tickets hidden within random bars of chocolate, the town erupts into a frenzy. One by one, tickets are claimed by fortunate recipients. Yet, amidst the jubilation, one ticket remains unclaimed. Luckily, Charlie finds a coin and purchases a bar of chocolate, scarcely daring to hope. Miraculously, he uncovers the final golden ticket. With his devoted Grandpa Joe by his side, Charlie then embarks on an extraordinary adventure as they enter the fantastical realm of Wonka's factory, a whimsical world filled with eccentric inventions and enchanting surprises.

Chitty Chitty Bang Bang
Author: Ian Fleming   Publication Date: 22nd October 1964

After inventing a novel musical chewing gum, former Royal Navy commander Caractacus Pott earns a substantial monetary windfall. He successfully sells his creation to Lord Skrumshus, a wealthy local confectionery factory owner. Eager to treat his family, Pott invests in a dilapidated car with the intention of restoring it to its former glory. After weeks of work, Pott's efforts culminate in a stunning transformation. The car boasts a pristine chrome exterior, luxurious red leather upholstery, and an array of intricate buttons and knobs. Commander and Mrs. Pott, along with their twins Jeremy and Jemima, embark on a journey in the newly restored vehicle. Jeremy coins the name "Chitty-Chitty-Bang-Bang" after the car's distinctive sounds. However, this is no ordinary car, as it unexpectedly sprouts wings and takes flight like an airplane. With their newfound mode of transportation, the Pott family is poised for the adventure of a lifetime.

Harriet The Spy
Author: Louise Fitzhugh   First published in 1964

Harriet observes the world around her and documents everything she sees in her notebook. She spies on a range of people in her life and takes copious notes about the good, the bad and the tedious. She keeps tabs on her neighbours including the wealthy woman in her apartment building who lies in bed all day talking on the phone, the loud family that owns the corner grocery store and her friends. Harriet doesn't hold back in her notebooks and she gets into big trouble with her classmates when they read some of the more uncharitable lines she has written about them. Over the course of the novel, Harriet learns some tough lessons about how to balance her candid take on the world with her need for friendship. Though *Harriet the Spy* was published in the 1960s, the novel will still appeal to readers today, especially those who like a laugh and anyone trying to figure out how to be honest while maintaining friendships.

The Shot Marilyns

In 1964, Andy Warhol lived in his Factory in Manhattan, where he continued to produce silkscreens featuring Marilyn Monroe, an enduring subject of fascination for him. Among his latest creations were five canvases with Marilyn depicted against various coloured backgrounds, displayed in his studio. During a visit from two guests, Warhol's friend Billy Name introduced him to photographer Dorothy Podber, who expressed interest in 'shooting' the Marilyns. Assuming she meant photographing his artwork, Warhol granted her permission. However, Podber then removed her gloves, retrieved a revolver from her purse, and fired at the canvases, damaging four out of five. These works became known as the *Shot Marilyns*. Following the incident, Warhol reportedly requested that Podber refrain from such actions in the future and subsequently banned her from the Factory. The *Shot Marilyns*, now damaged, found their way into the hands of various collectors around the world, becoming highly sought-after pieces in Warhol's portfolio. Unfortunately, this was not the end of gun-related incidents in Warhol's life. In 1968, he was infamously shot twice by Valerie Solanas, an event that had lasting repercussions, requiring him to wear a surgical corset to support his internal organs for the remainder of his life. Four years later, in 1972, actor Dennis Hopper, spooked by a portrait of Mao on Warhol's wall, fired at one of his silkscreens. The Shot Sage Blue Marilyn, one of the iconic pieces damaged in the incident, was auctioned by Christie's in New York City on 9th May 2022, fetching a staggering $195 million.

The 1953 photo that Andy Warhol based his 'Shot Marilyn' silkscreen prints

Single Form

Single Form by Barbara Hepworth. Located in Battersea Park, London

Barbara Hepworth was one of the most pre-eminent sculptors of the twentieth century, with a career that spanned decades of tumultuous political and social change. She is best known as a carver and this is how she would often describe herself, although her artistic output also incorporated painting, drawing, fabric design, printmaking and making work in metal through various techniques. She was also a prolific writer, producing eloquent statements on her art and philosophy throughout her life. Several of these texts reflect upon her personal life and her broader cultural interests, from architecture, music and poetry to political activism, science and technological developments. In 1956, Dag Hammarskjöld, Secretary-General of the United Nations, selected one of Hepworth's sculptures for his office, starting a correspondence that became a friendship due in part to their shared commitment to the cause of peace. In September 1960 Hammarskjöld was killed in a plane crash. Hepworth created several sculptures in his memory, culminating in the monumental *Single Form* (1964), permanently situated outside the UN headquarters in New York. Its shield-like form is comprised of many parts and recalls neolithic standing stones providing, as Hepworth described: "a symbol of both continuity and solidarity for the future."

John Masefield, Poet Laureate (served 1930-1967)

John Masefield

Masefield was the longest serving Poet Laureate to serve entirely within the 20th century. His 37 years of service was only beaten by Alfred, Lord Tennyson who held the post between 1850-1892. By the 1950s, Masefield seemed to be from a bygone era as traditional poetry had fallen out of favour as modernist poets such as Sylvia Plath and Stevie Smith were gaining traction. The emerging Beat Generation of poets such as Ginsburg, Carr and Huncke seemed to speak more to the youth of the day than did the rather staid Masefield. Still, he took his job seriously and acted as all good Poets Laureate do. He wrote poems for the court, in his case the House of Windsor. Rather quaintly Masefield would send his poems to The Times of London for their approval with a stamped addressed envelope for their response. Even though he seemed more like a 19th century poet than most of his contemporaries, many of his poems still stand the test of time. His *Sonnets and Poems* written in the midst of World War I and *A Generation Risen* written during World War II defined him as a chronicler of British 20th century history and one of the few poets to have written during both wars. In 1964, Masefield published his penultimate collection of poems, *Old Raiger and Other Verses.* He died three years later in 1967.

The Role of Poet Laureate Through The Ages

The monarch of the day bestows the honorary position of Poet Laureate, currently on the advice of the prime minister. There are no specific duties to the role although it is expected that the holder produces original verse to commemorate significant national occasions. The first official Poet Laureate was John Dryden who was appointed by Charles II in 1668. Until Andrew Motion was appointed in 1999, the laureateship was held for life; subsequently the position has been offered for a fixed term of 10 years. Other notable Poet Laureates included William Wordsworth (1843-1850), Sir John Betjeman (1972-1984) and Ted Hughes (1984-1998). The actor Daniel Day-Lewis's father, Cecil, was also Poet Laureate from 1968 to 1972. It was only in 2009 that the first woman, Carol Ann Duffy, was offered the role. She was also the first Scot.

Sir John Betjeman

The role of Poet Laureate is not a money spinner; Andrew Motion and Carol Ann Duffy were offered annual salaries of £5,750 per year. However, in a quirky tradition dating back to Charles I, the holder also receives a barrel of sherry.

Carol Ann Duffy

The First Close Up Images of the Moon's Surface

The first close up picture of the moon

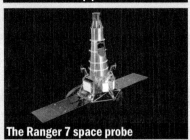
The Ranger 7 space probe

The NASA Ranger program was set up with the goal of obtaining close-up images of the surface of the moon. The plan was to launch an uncrewed probe and crash it into the lunar surface, capturing images and video in the last few minutes before impact. The program proved much more problematic than expected. In fact, Ranger missions 1-6 all failed with some probes experiencing technical problems with their equipment whilst others completely failed to hit the moon altogether. In July 1964, Ranger 7 was launched on-board an Atlas-Agena B rocket. After a mid journey course correction, Ranger 7 reached the moon on the 31st July. It's six cameras captured over 4,300 images of the lunar surface during the final 17 minutes before impact. The pictures gave scientists their first indications that the moon's surface may be suitable for humans to safely land on. Ranger missions 8 and 9 were also successful and gathered thousands more images to confirm this. The Ranger 7 mission is also noted for being the origin of NASA's 'peanut' tradition. At the moment the mission was deemed a success, it was noted someone in mission control was eating peanuts. Since 1964, NASA control rooms ceremonially open a bag of peanuts for luck and tradition.

The Discovery of Cosmic Microwave Background Radiation

In the middle decades of the 20th century, there were two competing theories as to how the universe was formed. One was a 'steady-state' theory suggesting that the universe has always existed and will fundamentally remain without major alteration. The alternative hypothesis was the Big Bang Theory. In this, the universe was created billions of years ago through a gigantic explosion event. Part of the theory required a prediction of cosmic microwave background (CMB) radiation. In the 1940s, the prominent cosmologist George Gamow and colleagues predicted the existence of CMB radiation in space on the basis that during the the the early moments of the universe, it was extremely hot and dense. As the universe expanded, it cooled down, leaving behind a faint afterglow of radiation namely CMB. However, at this time, scientific instruments were not capable of detecting it so it remained a hypothesis. In 1964, American physicist Arno Penzias and radio-astronomer Robert Wilson made the groundbreaking discovery of detecting CMB using the Holmdel Horn Antenna. After removing all other sources of noise they detected a steady, faint radiation which they believed came from outside our galaxy. It bore out the earlier predictions from Gamow and others and gave credibility to the Big Bang Theory. We have subsequently learned that the Big Bang event took place some 13.8 billion years ago. In 1978, Penzias and Wilson were awarded the Nobel Prize for Physics.

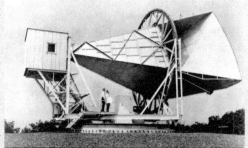
The Holmdel Horn Antenna used in New Jersey

The Birth of the European Space Research Organisation (ESRO)

The European Space Research Organisation (ESRO) was formed in 1964 as an international collaboration between 10 European nations. These were France, Belgium, Italy, Denmark, (Federal Republic of) Germany, Spain, Netherlands, Switzerland, Sweden and the United Kingdom. ESRO's primary objective was to advance scientific research in space. Inspired by the success of the European Organisation for Nuclear Research (CERN), two influential physicists, Edoardo Amaldi from Italy and Pierre Victor Auger from France, played pivotal roles in shaping ESRO. Their vision was to create a unified organisation where European countries could pool their expertise, resources, and scientific curiosity to explore the cosmos. In its 11-year history, ESRO launched several successful satellite and space missions. Notable among them was the Aurora 7 mission in 1971, which carried French astronaut Claude Nicollier into space. ESRO's satellites collected important data on solar radiation, atmospheric composition, and magnetic fields leading to breakthrough discoveries about our atmosphere and the broader universe. In 1975, ESRO merged with ELDO (European Launcher Development Organisation) to form ESA (European Space Agency) to continue and broaden ESRO's work.

The ESRO-2 Mission Control Room in Germany

Voskhod 1

The Russian Voskhod 1 space mission launched on the 12th October 1964 from the Baikonur Cosmodrome in Kazakhtstan. It was notable for three world firsts. It was the first spaceflight to carry more than one crew member. It was also the first human spaceflight where the crew did not wear spacesuits. Finally, it was the first spaceflight to carry an engineer or physician. For the mission, cosmonaut and command pilot Vladimir Komarov was joined on-board by engineer Konstantin Feoktistov and medical doctor Boris Yegorov. They shared a tiny command capsule which, due to its cramped conditions, did not allow the cosmonauts to wear bulky spacesuits. Voskhod 1, which translates to Sunshine 1, had an anticipated mission length of just over 24 hours. A lot happened in that time. Firstly the crew set a new altitude record reaching 336km (209 miles) above the Earth's surface. More extraordinary was that the crew left earth with one Soviet premier in charge of the country and landed with another. Soon after launch, the incumbant premier Nikita Khrushchev spoke to the crew from Crimea. After that conversation, he was summoned back to Moscow where he learned he was being expelled from office and the communist party. The crew returned to be greeted by Leonid Brezhnev and Alexei Kosygin in their first appearance as new leaders of the country.

The Voskhod 1 capsule

The Unisphere (centre) became the symbol of the Fair

25 years after the last World's Fair in New York and marking the 300th anniversary of the naming of the city, the 1964 New York World's Fair opened to the public on the 22nd April. Staged on the same site as the 1939/40 Fair at Flushing Meadows-Corona Park, the Fair was conceived by a group of local businessmen who remembered visiting the earlier Fair when they were children. Keen to boost the local economy, the group submitted their plans to the Bureau of International Expositions (BIE) in Paris for approval. However, they were turned down due to rules not allowing the same country to hold a Fair within 10 years of a previous one. It was only 2 years earlier that Seattle had held an official World's Fair. In addition, the New York plans required that the Fair be run for two six-month stints in order to turn a profit; BIE rules only allow a fair to run for six months total. As a result, the 1964 New York World's Fair is the only one to have gone ahead without official endorsement. To make matters worse for the organisers, the BIE asked its international members not to participate. The result was that the Fair was dominated by American exhibitors. International pavilions and stands were present but these were typically supplied by smaller, non-BIE member countries such as the Vatican City, the Philippines and Ireland. With a lack of major cultural stands from other countries there was more of a focus on it being a consumer show, showcasing new products in technology, living and transportation.

The Flushing Meadows site was originally a wetland area alongside the Flushing river. In the early 1900's it was used as a garbage dump. The vision to turn it into a park for city residents was one of the grandest designs of the influential New York city urban planner, Robert Moses. That vision was mostly realised for the 1939 Fair, however that show made a loss meaning that the Park was never finished. Moses, who was also involved in the 1964 Fair, saw this as a chance to complete his work. The theme of the 1964 Fair was 'Peace Through Understanding' symbolised by the 12-storey high 'Unisphere'. This stainless steel representation of the earth sat on the same pedestal as the 180 feet wide 'Perisphere' used in the 1939 Fair. The Unisphere has three rings around the earth which represent the first man-made satellites to orbit the Earth. Although it eventually fell into to disrepair, the Unisphere was restored in the 2010s and is now protected as an official designated landmark. The architecture of the 1964 World's Fair was in the futurist style known as Googie architecture. With influences including car culture, jets, the Atomic Age and the Space Age, the unusual name derives from Googies Coffee Shop in Hollywood, California designed by John Lautner. The main United States pavilion featured a 15-minute ride through a filmed presentation of American history. The pavilion also featured a tribute to the late John F. Kennedy who had visited the site in December 1962, 11 months before his assassination. The New York State pavilion was a $6 million open air 'Tent of Tomorrow' designed by famed modernist architect, Phillip Johnson. Alongside it were the fair's three tall observation towers. Wisconsin's pavilion included the 'World's Largest Cheese'. Industry pavilions included companies such as General Motors, IBM, DuPont and The Chunky Candy Corporation. The Ford pavilion is where the company launched its new Ford Mustang model. It also included Ford's 'Magic Skyway' ride where guests rode in convertible cars past scenes starting in prehistoric times and finishing with a city of the future. Of the international pavilions, the Vatican City's was one of the most popular as it included Michaelanglelo's *Pietà* sculpture. Belgium's recreation of a medieval village was also popular, probably due to the serving of a specially created waffle. Walt Disney also featured prominently throughout the Fair where his company created four shows featuring lifelike robots acting out scenes. Disney did consider the idea of turning the Fair's site into an East Coast Disneyland but it didn't materialise. However the concept was used as the blueprint for Epcot which opened in Florida in 1982. Despite attracting over 51 million visitors the Fair's organisers had banked on 70 million meaning that, like the 1939 Fair, financially it made a loss. However, many Baby Boomers, who visited it as children, remember an optimistic and exciting spectacular.

The Chrysler Capitol Pavilion

The Johnson Wax Pavilion

Walt Disney perfected his Audio-Animatronics at the Fair. A lifelike Abraham Lincoln recited speeches at the Illinois pavilion

The Space Park

US Royal's 'Giant Tire' Ferris Wheel

The Lockheed SR-71 Blackbird

On the 22nd December 1964 at a classified USAF manufacturing facility in Palmdale, California, pilot Bob Gilliland made the first ever flight in Lockheed's extraordinary reconnaissance aircraft, the SR-71 'Blackbird'. As a development from their top secret Skunk Works division, this Lockheed aircraft could reach speeds exceeding Mach 3. During test flights it reached speeds of Mach 3.3 which is in excess of 2,000mph! As well as incredible speed, the Blackbird was also designed to operate at extremely high altitudes, often cruising at 80,000 feet or more. The aircraft would play a crucial role during the Cold War, providing valuable intelligence flying high over

The SR-71 flying over the Sierra Nevada Mountains

enemy territories. The SR-71 was constructed primarily using titanium, chosen for its strength at high temperatures. This posed significant challenges during manufacturing due to the scarcity of the material and the advanced fabrication techniques required. Pilots would wear special suits which were akin to space suits as they needed to function in a near vacuum environment. The plane was so fast that if an enemy launched a surface-to-air missile, the pilot would simply accelerate and outrun it. It holds the record for flying between New York and London in 1h 54mins. For comparison, Concorde's fastest flight was 2h 52mins.

The Bell Aerosystems Lunar Landing Research Vehicle

Lunar Landing Research Vehicle No. 2 in flight

In September 1962, President John F. Kennedy gave his famous speech declaring that the USA would go to the moon. For the Apollo Moon landings that were to follow, NASA would require a vehicle to simulate lunar landings for astronauts to train on. The design needed to be capable of simulating the Moon's low gravity environment. Bell Aerosystems's answer to this was problem was the LLRV (Lunar Landing Research Vehicle). Striking in it's appearance, it consisted of a turbo fan jet engine, used for executive jets, centrally mounted on a gimbel that would keep the engine pointed downwards even if the frame was at an angle. The thrust of the jet engine could be set to compensate for 5/6 of the vehicles total weight thus simulating the Moon's gravity. The pilot of the LLRV then had control over additional hydrogen peroxide rockets which could be fired at different thrusts and in different directions to provide flight control. Should anything go wrong, the vehicle was also fitted with the world's first zero-zero ejection seat which meant that the pilot could eject at very low altitudes and be thrust high enough in the air for a parachute to deploy and safely land. Five vehicles were built, of which 3 were crashed during test flights, including a flight by Neil Armstrong. However, everyone ejected safely. Apollo astronauts cite the LLRV as the unsung here of the Apollo missions in providing the vital training of landing the lunar module on the Moon's surface.

The Mikoyan-Gurevich MiG-25

A two-seat trainer MiG-25PU

During the Cold War, Soviet Air Defence Forces were tasked with strategically defending the USSR against US reconnaissance aircraft and strategic bombers. The need for improved interceptor aircraft became particularly evident in the late 1950s, prompted by the very high altitude overflights of Soviet territory by the US Lockheed U-2 spy plane. In 1939, aircraft designers Artem Mikoyan and Mikhail Gurevich formed the Mikoyan and Gurevich Design Bureau, or 'MiG' for short. Since that date, their aircraft designs provided the majority of the fighter and interceptor aircraft for the Soviet Air Force. The MiG-25 would be the last aircraft designed by Mikhail Gurevich before his retirement. It was an extraordinary piece of engineering and would become one of the fastest military aircraft to ever enter service. The prototype first flew on 6th March 1964. Featuring a highly advanced radar system and four air-to-air missiles, the MiG-25 was capable of cruising speeds above Mach 3 at altitudes above 80,000 feet. It was in production until 1984, by which time nearly 1,200 aircraft had been built. It has held numerous aviation records including the absolute altitude record for a jet aircraft under its own power. In 1977, Soviet test pilot Aleksandr Fedotov flew his MiG-25 in a zoom climb to 123,520 feet, way up into the stratosphere.

The North American XB-70 Valkyrie

Conceived in the depths of the Cold War, the XB-70 Valkyrie was designed as a high-altitude nuclear bomber capable of delivering nuclear payloads deep into enemy territory. With its distinctive delta wing design, the XB-70 was capable of flying at 70,000 feet at speeds over Mach 3 making it virtually impossible to detect and intercept. It was equipped with six turbojet engines attached at the rear of the delta shaped airframe. The maiden flight on the 21st September 1964 between Palmdale and Edwards Air Force Base in California was beset with problems. One of the engines needed to

The XB-70 on a test flight with a chase plane in pursuit

be shut down straight after takeoff. Problems with the undercarriage meant that the wheels were kept down during the flight. Upon landing one of the tyres ruptured causing a fire. However, worse was to come. In 1966, during a photoshoot with the XB-70 flying in close formation with four other aircraft, an F-104 supersonic Starfighter accidentally clipped wings with the XB-70. The Starfighter flipped over on top of the XB-70 then exploded, destroying the Valkyrie's stabiliser. The XB-70 then crashed to the ground. This disaster along with other challenges, including cost overruns and the evolving nature of strategic requirements, lead to the programme's cancellation in 1969.

Donald Campbell's World Records

The son of Sir Malcolm Campbell, Donald was born on the 23rd March 1921. Donald's early attempts at records began with the World Water Speed Record. He used the boat Bluebird K4 for his early forays, but despite some valiant efforts, he struggled with the boat his father had used. Donald suffered a 170 mph crash in 1951 which prompted him to develop a completely new boat which became known as the K7. This was to prove a formidable boat which saw Donald Campbell set 7 World Water Speed Records between 1955 and 1964. The first record was set at Ullswater under the shadow of Mount Helvellyn in England's Lake District, with a speed of 202 mph. This was raised to 216 mph in 1958 and then 276 mph at Lake Dumbleyoung, Western Australia, in 1964. Donald's attention also involved cars and while

A painting of Donald Campbell

attempting a record run in Utah during 1960, he crashed heavily resulting in injury and a long period of convalescence. It was at this time that people questioned his abilities. In 1964, Donald put all questions to rest setting a new World Land Speed Record of 403mph at Lake Eyre. Unsuccessfully attempting the 'Unique Double' at Lake Bonney in Southern Australia, Campbell moved on to Lake Dumbleyoung and successfully recorded a 276.3 mph World Water Speed Record thus achieving the unique feat of holding simultaneous World Speed Records.

Bluebird K7 pictured in 1960

Donald was the first and only person to this day to hold both Water and Land Speed Records at the same time. Three years later on 4th January 1967, while attempting to break the 300 mph speed barrier on water, Donald crashed at Coniston Water. After achieving a speed of 297 mph on the first leg, Donald Campbell set off on the second leg not waiting for the wake to settle. Exceeding the speed of 300 mph, the nose of the Bluebird lifted out of the water. The boat somersaulted and disintegrated on impact with the water's surface. The great Donald Campbell was killed instantly. For many years it was believed that Campbell and his boat were lost forever but the wreckage was raised by Bill Smith's dive team on 8th March 2001. Campbell's body was recovered on 28th May that year and he was buried in the village on 12th September. The Ruskin museum was gifted the wreckage in 2006 by his daughter, Gina Campbell, on the understanding Mr. Smith would restore it at his workshop in North Shields. A museum spokesman said "an agreement has been reached" which would see the craft returned to Coniston in the near future. "Bluebird will be back within a stone's throw of its skipper who is buried in the village. It is right and proper that it is there." In February 2024 it was confirmed that the restored Bluebird K7 would finally return to Coniston to be displayed in the Bluebird Wing of the Ruskin Museum.

Bluebird CN7 sets the record on Lake Eyre in 1964

The Trial of the Great Train Robbers

The trial began on 20th January 1964 at Aylesbury courthouse before Justice Edmund Davies. During proceedings Jack Mills, the train driver, took the stand. Still recovering from the effects of his head injury, he recounted the episode in detail, giving attention to the injuries he had sustained at the hands of the robbers. Due to the fact that robbery suspect Biggs had previously been in prison, his presence in court was deemed as breaching impartiality and he was sent back to prison. Another suspect John Daly craftily had his lawyer make a submission to the court that a Monopoly set, which belonged to him, could have had his fingerprints on it before it was taken to the farm where the gang were arrested. The jury agreed and Daly was acquitted. On 23rd March 1964, the jury retired for two days to consider their verdicts. Tom Wisbey, Roy James, Charlie Wilson, Bob Welch, Jim Hussey and Gordon Goody were all found guilty

Ronnie Biggs

of the train robbery. Sentencing was delayed until after Biggs' retrial, which was set for 8th April 1964. Finally sentencing was passed. All the men, including Biggs, each received

Bruce Reynolds in 1999

between 24 and 30 years in prison. Most of the gang were sent to Brixton prison. Biggs went to Wandsworth prison, also in South London. On 12th August while Biggs was plotting an escape, Charlie Wilson absconded from Winson Green prison in Birmingham, with the assistance of three unidentified accomplices. On Thursday 8th July 1965 Biggs and fellow prisoner, Eric Flower, exploited the lax security around their exercise yard and escaped over the perimeter wall when rope ladders were thrown over. The plan had been arranged for some time on the outside. Biggs and Flower were hidden in various parts of the country for several months before being smuggled across the English Channel to Antwerp in Belgium. There Biggs underwent plastic surgery to hide his identity, as well as being given money, a new passport and clothes. Travelling to Australia under the alias Terrence Furminger, he was reunited with his family and Eric Flower. He spent several years hiding out in various places around the country. In 1968 Bruce Reynolds, Charlie Wilson and Jimmy White were all arrested and each given long terms in jail. 'Buster' Edwards eventually gave himself up to the police. Biggs was the only known member of the gang who remained free. Realising the net was closing in, he scraped some money together, borrowed a passport and booked a passage to Panama. Once there he took a flight to Rio de Janeiro via Caracas, Venezuela. On 11th March 1970, Biggs landed in Rio as 'Michael Haynes' and he gradually settled into life there. He still kept in constant touch with his wife and family and led a colourful eventful life, with many girlfriends. In May 2001, after 31 years in Brazil, Biggs, aged 71, returned to England. He was a very ill man, having suffered several strokes, but wanted to return even if it meant being re-imprisoned for his crimes. If he was expecting pity on the part of the law, he was sadly mistaken. He was arrested and later imprisoned despite a media campaign by family and friends calling for the Government to offer clemency. However, on 6th August 2009, with his health in decline, Biggs was released from prison on compassionate grounds. He died on 18th December 2013.

The Great Alaskan Earthquake | Prince William Sound, Alaska

The 1964 earthquake that struck Prince William Sound in Alaska stands as the most powerful seismic event ever documented in North America. Its epicentre, located approximately 74 miles southeast of Anchorage, unleashed tremors felt across much of Alaska's mainland, with repercussions even reaching as far as the Space Needle in Seattle, some 1,200 miles away. Notably, the quake resonated throughout all US states except for Delaware, Connecticut and Rhode Island. On Good Friday evening on the 27th March 1964, the earth started to shake at 5:36pm, catching many Alaskans mid-dinner.

Fourth Avenue in Anchorage after the landslide

Witnesses recounted a cacophony of crunching and grinding noises as the ground shook beneath them. Tarmac roads undulated like ocean waves, fissures tore through the terrain, and water spewed skyward from newly formed cracks. The violent upheaval ruptured water, sewer, and gas lines, while also causing widespread disruptions to telephone and electrical networks. Telephone poles tumbled, railroad tracks buckled and structures, vehicles, and docks were demolished. The seismic waves reverberated through the earth, creating an eerie 'ringing' sensation. As devastating as the initial tremors were, the true horror was still to come. The earthquake triggered a series of catastrophic tsunamis, landslides, and underwater avalanches, resulting in loss of life and massive damage to property. 131 people died, 15 during the initial tremors and the remainder succumbing to subsequent tsunamis and landslides. In a span of four minutes, coastal areas experienced dramatic shifts: some sank up to eight feet, others rose as much as 38 feet, while vast stretches extended 50 feet closer to the ocean. Forests along the coast were inundated by saltwater, leading to their destruction. The town of Valdez, situated on unstable sand and gravel, bore the brunt of the disaster. Seismic waves induced liquefaction, causing a portion of the delta to collapse into Port Valdez, dragging much of the port's infrastructure and resources with it. This delta slump triggered a local tsunami, exacerbating the destruction and igniting a massive fire

Terrifying force of the tsunami

when Union Oil Company's oil tanks ruptured. Valdez lay in ruins, with the largest tsunami wave measuring over 200 feet in height at Shoup Bay near the Valdez inlet. In the aftermath, thousands of aftershocks, some exceeding magnitude 6.2, continued for weeks. Reports emerged of residual water movements, or seiches, as far away as the US Gulf Coast and Australia. Scientists leveraged the wealth of data gathered to implement a comprehensive earthquake monitoring system aimed at predicting future seismic events and minimising their impact. This knowledge also guided engineers in designing earthquake-resistant structures, and the establishment of the Pacific Tsunami Warning Center to enhance early warning capabilities. The quake was the second largest ever recorded, the magnitude 9.5 event at Valdivia, Chile, in 1960 is the largest.

The Estadio Nacional Disaster

On 24th May 1964, tragedy struck the Peruvian capital Lima during a football match, marking one the deadliest stadium disasters in history. Over 300 people lost their lives in the chaos that ensued. While the complete picture of what happened remains elusive, piecing together accounts from multiple eyewitnesses offers some insight into the events that transpired. During a crucial match against Argentina in South America's Olympic qualifying tournament at the National Stadium of Peru, the home team found themselves in a high-stakes situation, needing at least a draw to secure their qualifying position in the group table. With a packed stadium of some 53,000 spectators, tensions

Fellow spectators carrying an injured fan to safety
Image courtesy of the Peruvian Institute of Sport

were running high as the game unfolded. Peru had the momentum playing strong, attacking football. However, Argentina took the lead against the run of play. Peruvian defender Hector Chumpitaz recollected the pivotal moment when frustration erupted among the crowd. A disallowed goal for Peru led to uproar, compounded by the incursion of two spectators onto the field. The first, a bouncer by the name of Bomba, attempted to attack the referee before being restrained by authorities and bundled off the field. The second, Edilberto Cuenca, experienced a serious assault by police, further inciting the crowd's anger. As the situation escalated, spectators began hurling projectiles at the authorities with more Peruvian fans attempting to break onto the field. Recognising the escalating danger, many other spectators opted to try and leave the stadium. However, they found themselves trapped when exit gates were closed, forcing them to turn around. However, just at this moment, the police started throwing tear gas at groups of marauding supporters. Chaos ensued as thousands in the stands tried to escape down stair wells and tunnels meeting fans who had already turned around due to the closed gates. Eyewitnesses recalled the horror and harrowing experience of the ensuing slow-moving human crush as tear gas filled the stands. Many people were severely crushed, some dying by asphyxiation. Some spectators spent as much as two hours trapped amidst a mass of bodies, some living, some deceased. One fan recalls that his feet did not touch the ground the whole time, such was the nature of the crush.

The Estadio Nacional was built in 1952

While the exact sequence of events may never be fully known, the 1964 Estadio Nacional disaster serves as a sombre reminder to the sporting world of the potential dangers of large-scale events and the vital importance of effective crowd management and safety protocols.

The Warren Commission Report is Published

The Warren Commission in session

Lee Harvey Oswald

Earl Warren hands President Johnson the report

The President's Commission on the assassination of President Kennedy, known unofficially as the Warren Commission, was established by President Lyndon B. Johnson on 29th November 1963 to probe the assassination of United States President John F. Kennedy that had taken place on 22nd November, 1963. The 88th US Congressional session passed Senate joint resolution 137 authorising the Presidential appointed Commission to report on the assassination, mandating the attendance and testimony of witnesses and the production of evidence concerning the atrocity that occurred in Dallas, Texas. Its 889-page final report was presented to Kennedy's successor, President Johnson on 24th September 1964 and made public three days later. It concluded that President Kennedy was assassinated by Lee Harvey Oswald and that Oswald acted alone. It concluded that Jack Ruby had also acted alone when he killed Oswald two days later. The Commission took its unofficial name, the Warren Commission, from its chairman, Chief Justice Earl Warren. In November 1964, two months after the publication of its report, the Commission published twenty-six volumes of supporting documents, including the testimony or depositions of 552 witnesses and more than 3,100 exhibits. All of the commission's records were then transferred on 23rd November to the National Archives. The unpublished portion of those records was initially sealed for 75 years (to 2039) under a general National Archives policy that applied to all federal investigations by the executive branch of government, a period "intended to serve as protection for innocent persons who could otherwise be damaged because of their relationship with participants in the case." The 75-year rule no longer exists, supplanted by the Freedom of Information Act of 1966 and the JFK Records Act of 1992. By 1992, 98 percent of the Warren Commission records had been released to the public. Six years later, at the conclusion of the Assassination Records Review Board's work, all Warren Commission records, except those that contained tax return information, were available to the public with redactions. In October 2017, the National Archives released more than 2,800 previously classified records relating to the assassination. The documents sparked a feeding frenzy among historians and conspiracy theorists alike. Among the revelations to emerge from the files were CIA notes on an intercepted telephone call on 28th September 1963, from Lee Harvey Oswald to a KGB agent in Mexico City. There was also evidence that the FBI's Dallas office received a threat on Oswald's life on 23rd November 1963, the night before Jack Ruby shot him, from a man saying he was a "member of a committee organised to kill Oswald." Many of the most anticipated remaining files relate to a trip Oswald took to Mexico City in September 1963, just two months before he shot Kennedy. During his visit, Oswald went to the Cuban embassy and met with officials in his attempt to get a visa to travel to Cuba, and then on to the Soviet Union.

The Rivonia Trial

On the 12th June 1964, Nelson Mandela and seven of his comrades were sentenced to life imprisonment during the historic Rivonia Trial. Alongside Mandela, Ahmed Kathrada, Walter Sisulu, Elias Motsoaledi, Andrew Mlangeni, Govan Mbeki, Raymond Mhlaba, and Denis Goldberg were found guilty of sabotage by Judge Quartus. All except Denis Goldberg, the sole white defendant, were transported in chains to Robben Island Maximum Security Prison, while Goldberg was held at Pretoria Central Prison for the next 21 years due to apartheid regulations governing prisoner treatment. The long trial had started back in October 1963. Facing the possibility of a death sentence, Mandela chose to deliver a statement from the dock rather than testify. His memorable words, spoken during a four-hour speech on 20th April 1964, encapsulated his lifelong dedication to the struggle against racial oppression:

Mandela burning his pass in an act of defiance in 1960

"During my lifetime, I have dedicated myself to this struggle of the African people. I have fought against white domination and black domination. I have cherished the ideal of a democratic and free society in which all persons live together in harmony and with equal opportunities. It is an ideal for which I hope to live and to achieve. But if needs be, it is an ideal for which I am prepared to die." By the time of his sentencing, Mandela had already been serving a five-year prison term on Robben Island since 7th November 1962 for unlawful departure from the country and incitement of worker strikes, when his comrades were arrested at Liliesleaf Farm in the Johannesburg suburb of Rivonia. He had been underground since April 1961, travelling without an official passport to various African countries and the

The room on Liliesleaf Farm in Rivonia where the ANC activists were arrested

United Kingdom before his arrest in Howick, KwaZulu-Natal, on 5th August 1962. During the Rivonia Trial, Mandela used his time in the dock to narrate the history of racial oppression in South Africa and to justify the African National Congress's transition to armed resistance after exhausting peaceful means of protest. He remained incarcerated on Robben Island until March 1982 when he was transferred to Pollsmoor Prison in Cape Town. His health deteriorated in 1988 due to tuberculosis, leading to treatment at Tygerberg Hospital in Bellville and Constantiaberg Medi-Clinic before his relocation to Victor Verster Prison in Paarl. Denis Goldberg was released in 1985, followed by Govan Mbeki in 1987, and the remaining comrades in 1989. Just over three months later, on 11th February 1990, Nelson Mandela finally walked out of the gates of Victor Verster Prison, marking the beginning of a new era for South Africa. On 9th May 1994, Mandela was elected as the first president of South Africa's post-apartheid era. Verifiable statistics on the human cost of apartheid are scarce and estimates vary. However, in his often-cited book *A Crime Against Humanity*, Max Coleman of the Human Rights Committee places the number of deaths due to political violence during the apartheid era as high as 21,000. These were almost exclusively black deaths, most occurred during notorious bloodbaths such as the Sharpeville Massacre of 1960 and the Soweto Student Uprising of 1976-1977.

The 1964 Innsbruck Air Disaster

A Bristol Britannia from British Eagle International Airlines, identical to the sister aircraft involved

On 4th March 1964 the Parliamentary Secretary at the Ministry of Aviation, Mr. Neil Marten stood before the House of Commons to make the following statement: "As the House will know, a Britannia aircraft of British Eagle International Airlines crashed during the approach to Innsbruck Airport on 29th February 1964. It was on a scheduled service with a crew of eight and seventy-five passengers. None of those on-board survived. I am sure, Mr. Speaker, that the House will wish to join me in expressing sympathy with the bereaved, and our thanks to all who under the most difficult mountain conditions sought the wrecked aircraft in the hope that there might be survivors. In addition our thanks are due to the United States Air Force for sending the specially equipped aircraft which first located the wreckage; and to other aircraft engaged in the search and to the Austrian Accidents Commission which is investigating the accident." At 2:12 pm the pilot of Flight 802/6 reported that the aircraft was flying at 10,000ft. That was to be the last communication that Austrian air traffic control received from the crew. At around 2:20pm the Bristol Britannia 312 aircraft, crashed into the eastern slope of Glungezer, a mountain in the Austrian Tyrol, south-east of Innsbruck. Everyone on-board the aircraft including 81 Britons (most of whom were either going to the Winter Olympics or on a skiing holiday), one Austrian, and one Canadian were killed in the crash. A subsequent avalanche caused crash debris to move over 1000ft down the mountain. The recovery of the bodies and wreckage was hampered by the extremely difficult terrain which was accessible only by helicopter. Due to poor weather and lack of light, the wreckage was not located until the day after the crash. Five members of a Paisley family lost their lives on that date in 1964 as they headed for a once in a lifetime trip to the Winter Olympic Games in Innsbruck. It was in February 1964 that Bill Paterson, 47, went home to Huntly Terrace in Paisley from his job as a driver with the British Eagle airline, with the news that the company had given him and his family flights to Innsbruck to see the Winter Olympic Games. His wife Agnes, 43, daughter Nan, 20, and sons Billy, 14 and Campbell 10, excitedly prepared for the trip, scheduled for Saturday, 29th February 1964. The family never made it back home. Barbara Pearson who lost her aunt, uncle and three cousins in the crash, reflected some years later on the devastating effect the disaster had on her family: "I remember the worst thing about the time was that we just didn't know what had happened. There were no lines of communication, nothing...we were in the dark." An investigation concluded that the pilot had intentionally descended below the minimum safe altitude of 11,000ft.

Dorothy Crowfoot Hodgkin | 1964 Nobel Prize in Chemistry

Dorothy Crowfoot Hodgkin

Headlines like "Oxford Housewife Wins Nobel Prize" captured the attention of tabloid readers in 1964 as they announced Dorothy Hodgkin's groundbreaking achievement. Hodgkin became the first British woman to receive a Nobel prize in science, lauded for her revolutionary techniques in visualising biomolecules using X-rays. Her contributions were monumental, leading to a profound understanding of the three-dimensional structure of penicillin, the first antibiotic. Despite her remarkable scientific prowess, Hodgkin found herself confronted with gender stereotypes during interviews, where she was often questioned about balancing her career with her domestic responsibilities. However, Hodgkin, raised with the belief that a fulfilling life encompassed both intellectual pursuits and personal growth, challenged such assumptions. Born in Cairo, where her father served in the Ministry of Education, Hodgkin's upbringing was marked by frequent travels between Egypt, England, and Sudan, amidst the backdrop of the First World War. Her fascination with minerals and the intricate geometries of crystalline structures began in her youth. At the age of twelve, during a visit to Sudan to accompany her father's archaeological endeavours, Hodgkin's curiosity was piqued by a particularly intriguing mineral. Her inquiry led to a transformative gift from a family friend, scientist A.F. Joseph: a mineral analysis kit. This pivotal moment ignited Hodgkin's passion for scientific inquiry, eventually culminating in the highest accolade in the scientific community, the Nobel Prize.

Martin Luther King Jr. | 1964 Nobel Peace Prize

Martin Luther King Jr.

Martin Luther King Jr. envisioned a United States of America where individuals would be judged on their character rather than the colour of their skin. Tragically, in April 1968, he was killed by a white supremacist. Four years prior in 1964, King had been honoured with the Nobel Peace Prize for his unwavering commitment to nonviolent resistance against racism, inspired by the principles of Gandhi. King's activism commenced in 1955, as he embarked on a crusade to challenge the legality of racial segregation in the southern states of the US. Despite advocating for nonviolent methods, he and other black activists encountered violent opposition from racist factions. In 1963, a pivotal moment occurred when 250,000 demonstrators converged on the Lincoln Memorial in Washington, D.C., where King delivered his iconic "I have a dream" speech. The following year, President Johnson successfully championed legislation through Congress to outlaw racial discrimination. However, King faced formidable adversaries, including FBI director J. Edgar Hoover, who surveilled him under the guise of communist affiliation. Additionally, King's outspoken opposition to the Vietnam War strained his relationship with the administration. The circumstances surrounding King's assassination remain shrouded in uncertainty, with speculation of potential conspiratorial involvement. Nonetheless, in 1986, Martin Luther King Jr. Day was established, commemorating his legacy on the third Monday of January near his birthday.

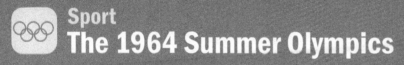

Games of the XVIII Olympiad | Tokyo 10th– 24th October 1964

Yoshinori Sakai with the torch | **Larysa Latynina** | **Lynn Davies** | **Mary Rand**

The 1964 Tokyo Games were the first to be held in Asia. The carrier of the flame, Yoshinori Sakai, was chosen because he was born on 6th August 1945, the day the atomic bomb was dropped on Hiroshima. This ceremonial homage to the victims marked a call for world peace. Although he never competed in an Olympics, two years later he won a gold medal in the 4 × 400 m relay and a silver in the 400 m at the 1966 Asian Games. A cinder running track was used for the last time in the athletics events, whilst a fibreglass pole was used for the first time in the pole vaulting competition. The Tokyo Games was also the last occasion that hand timing by stopwatch was used for official timing. Abebe Bikila of Ethiopia became the first athlete to win the marathon twice, whilst Soviet gymnast Larysa Latynina brought her career medal total to an incredible 18. It also proved fourth time lucky for Hungarian Greco-Roman wrestler Imre Polyak, who finally won gold after finishing second in the same division at the previous three Olympic Games.

Welsh long jumper and British record holder Lynn Davis was not among the favourites to win the gold medal at the Tokyo Games. Despite his making the final after qualifying with the second-longest jump, very few people gave the British athlete a chance against the defending champion, American Ralph Boston or even the Soviet/Ukrainian Ter-Ovanesyan. However on the day of the final, Davies won gold with a jump of 8.07m, ending a run of eight consecutive USA victories in the men's Olympic long jump competition. Davies credited his victory to the rainy, cold conditions in Japan, which he felt favoured his performance, likening them to the weather back home in Wales.

Mary Rand, one of Great Britain's finest ever female athletes, grew up fascinated with Japan. Then aged 24, she travelled to Tokyo, embraced every aspect of the local culture and returned home weeks later with a complete medal haul comprising one gold, one silver and one bronze. First up, the long jump. Rand broke the Olympic record in qualifying and never looked back. In the final, she landed great jump after great jump before, on her fifth effort, she soared out to 6.76m, a new world record. One gold and one world record in the bag, Rand turned her attention to the pentathlon. A gruelling event for most, but a relative stroll for the almost comically gifted Rand, who was at one time the British record holder in the

Games of the XVIII Olympiad | Tokyo 10th – 24th October 1964

Bob Hayes (far right) winning the 100m gold medal

Dick Thompson

80m hurdles, the long jump and the pentathlon as well as the owner of the unofficial women's triple jump world record. Rand won three of the five events in the pentathlon, but eventually had to settle for silver after dropping 384 points to the USSR's Irina Press in the shot put. The by now ever-smiling superstar completed the Olympic medal set by snatching bronze in the 4x100m relay. Tokyo 1964 made Rand a genuine superstar. Meetings with The Beatles followed, and The Rolling Stones' Mick Jagger even famously declared Rand to be his "dream date".

Bob Hayes was the most famous athlete to emerge from the Tokyo games. He won the 100 metres in a world record equalling 10.0 seconds, but it was in the relay that he really shone. Hayes, who was trailing by 4 metres when he received the baton, won the race by 3 metres covering his leg in an estimated 8.6 seconds. Hayes would go on to be known as the 'world's fastest human' with world records in the 60-yard, 100-yard, 220-yard and 100-metres. He then became a leading gridiron player for the Dallas Cowboys playing 11 seasons.

Tokyo also hosted their first Paralympic Games. The Games were held over just five days between 8th - 12th November. This was the second ever Paralympic Games after Rome 1960 but the first time the Paralympic name had been used. However, it was only a nickname used by the organising committee as the event was known as the 13th International Stoke Mandeville Games. So named after the British hospital that had hosted disability sports since the time of the London Olympics in 1948. Nine sports including archery, athletics, dartchery (a combination of darts and archery, which uses a dart board instead of a standard archery target), snooker, swimming, table tennis, weightlifting, wheelchair basketball and wheelchair fencing featured across six venues. The United States headed the medal table with 123 medals including 50 golds. Great Britain came second with 61 medals including 18 golds. Hosts Japan left the games with a solitary gold when they won the men's doubles in table tennis. It was a good games for Dick Thompson, the man who is widely regarded as the grandfather of the British Paralympic movement. He won 2 golds, a silver and two bronze medals in events as diverse as javelin, the wheelchair dash and the pentathlon.

12th August 1964 | The People newspaper lead with a story about match fixing in football.

After a 13-year career as a journeyman footballer, Jimmy Gauld had retired in 1961 due to a leg injury. A brief spell with Everton was the highlight of his career, but it was outside the field of play that he would make the biggest waves. Corruption in Association Football was not a new thing, with some famous scandals having rocked the game as early as 1915. Gauld, fuelled by greed, linked up with a betting syndicate who were seeking some quick cash by influencing the results of matches. His first target was a game between Sheffield Wednesday and Ipswich Town. Ipswich were the defending champions of the English League but they had found themselves languishing in the bottom three during the 1962 season. Wednesday meanwhile were in mid-table, but were having a tough time in their away fixtures. For this reason Ipswich were considered the favourites for the game. In order to fix the game, Gauld enlisted some inside help by approaching Sheffield's

Jimmy Gauld whilst at Everton

Football programme from the 1962 Ipswich Town v Sheffield Wednesday game
Image credit: 10footballs.com

David Layne, with whom he had played at Swindon Town. Layne in turn brought in teammates Tony Kay and Peter Swan. All went to plan and Wednesday lost 2-0. The three Sheffield players backed a win for Ipswich and won around £150. The next target for Gauld and his syndicate was a game between Bradford Park Avenue and Bristol Rovers on 20th April 1963. This time he recruited Keith Williams and Esmond Million of Bristol Rovers. He also influenced games involving Mansfield Town by 'signing up' their centre half Brian Phillips. However, rumours had begun to circulate regarding match fixing in lower leagues. Two journalists from the Sunday People, Mike Gabbert and Peter Campling, began investigating in August 1963. They exposed Ken Thomson of Hartlepool United for helping to fix a match between his team and Exeter City earlier in the year. The duo would then name Gauld as the mastermind of the whole affair. Aware that the game was up, Gauld sought to make an extra kill and decided to come clean on the whole affair in exchange for a large fee. He gave a tell-it-all interview to Gabbert and Campling in 1964 and the taped conversation would be a crucial piece of evidence in the subsequent trials. He exposed more players involved in fixing additional matches, demonstrating that his scheme was much more extensive than was initially thought. In January 1965, ten players including Gauld faced trial. Gauld being the ringleader was handed a 4-year sentence while the others were sentenced to between four and fifteen months. A total of 33 players had faced trial for the scandal. Swan, Layne and Kay were considered the other big wigs of the scandal and were handed life bans from the sport by the Football Association. Swan's fall from grace was the greatest. He had already won 19 caps for England and was held in high regard by manager Alf Ramsey and would probably have been part of the squad for the 1966 World Cup. Following a change to the rules by the FA in 1971, Phillips, Layne and Swan successfully appealed their bans, but by then they were well past their prime and they did not make any contribution of note to their teams.

Wimbledon | The Ladies' Final

Over the first half of the 1960s, two women set the agenda and settled more big matches than any other players. They delighted galleries all over the world with their contrasting personalities yet similarly aggressive styles. They attacked each other's games unwaveringly and intelligently, and more often than not brought out the best in each other. Brazil's Maria Bueno and the Australian Margaret Smith were clearly the pre-eminent players of that era, taking the women's game into another realm, a slower but in many ways more captivating type of serve-and-volley tennis than that of the men. Bueno vs Smith matches were not to be missed. They added value to the major championships simply by turning up. By 1964, their rivalry was at its peak. Bueno, born in Sao Paulo in October 1939, was nearly three years older than Smith, whose birthplace was Albury, New South Wales in July 1942. Their rivalry captivated the tennis world, particularly at Wimbledon. Their 12th encounter in 1964 showcased the elegant finesse of Bueno against the renowned athleticism of the Australian. From 1961 to 1975, Smith triumphed in every significant competition, yet the Wimbledon title of 1964 eluded her grasp. As the final set unfolded, Smith held a 3-2 advantage with her service imminent. However, the poised Bueno seeded second, rose to the occasion stringing together four consecutive games to secure the title for the third and final time with a scoreline of 6-4 7-9 6-3. In 1976, Margaret Smith married Barry Court, assuming the title of Mrs. Margaret Court.

Margaret Smith

Maria Bueno

Wimbledon | The Gentleman's Tournament

On the opening day of the 1964 Wimbledon Championships, Abe Segal of South Africa was drawn to play the American Clark Graebner in the first round. The order of play for the first day allocated the match to Court 3. On that same day the team of umpires and line judges held their annual start of Championships cocktail party. Play began at 2pm on a sunny afternoon and was then held up when one of the line judges, Dorothy Cavis Brown, was found to be fast asleep. An attempt to wake her was made by one of the ball-boys team, Robbie Thornton, but he was unsuccessful. So Segal broke off from concentrating on his match, walked over to the official and tapped her on the shoulder which did the trick. Quite what John McEnroe or Ile Nastase, the great tormentors of umpires and line-judges would have made of it, one can only imagine! The match resumed, Segal won it 6-2, 4-6, 6-3, 6-4 and as a consequence of these events, Mrs. Cavis Brown was given a few days off from her duties. Segal went on to reach the quarter-finals unseeded and he was beaten by the American Chuck McKinley 6-3, 6-3, 4-6, 6-4. The Gentlemen's singles title was won by Roy Emerson who defeated Fred Stolle in four sets; as far as we know all of the line judges stayed awake.

Roy Emerson

Rugby Union

In January 1964, the All Blacks came to Murrayfield near the end of their long tour of the UK and France. They had won their internationals against Ireland narrowly 6-5 in Dublin, Wales more impressively 6-0 at Cardiff Arms Park and England convincingly 14-0 at Twickenham. The Grand Slam of victories against the four home nations was within the All Blacks' grasp. However, Scotland had a valuable 'warm-up' 10-0 victory against France in the first international of the 1964 International Championship and were expected to be competitive. The All Blacks side under the captaincy of prop Wilson Whineray was based on a fearsome pack of forwards supported by the formidable place kicking of their giant 17-stone full back Don Clarke. Ken Gray and Dennis Young in the front row, Colin Meads in the second row and a back row of John Graham, Brian Lochore and Kelvin Tremain provided weight and pace unequalled in world rugby at the time. If their backs were less individually impressive, they were nevertheless strong defensively and capable of flashes of inspiration. The Scottish side under the captaincy of prop Brian Neill was initially unchanged for its second match of the season but

All Blacks captain, Wilson Whineray

the selectors were forced to make a late change when Jim Shackleton was brought in to replace the injured Brian Henderson in the centre. The team contained four players who had made their debut against France but Stuart Wilson at full back, Peter Brown in the second row and Jim Telfer in the back row would become among the finest Scottish players of their generation. For ballast, Ian Laughland in the centre, Norman Bruce at hooker with David Rollo as his other prop, and Pringle Fisher at wing forward provided essential quality in this relatively inexperienced side. The 1964 clash in front of 70,000 spectators was the last major international match to end in a 0-0 draw, but the score line does not do justice to the excitement of the game itself. It was a frosty day and handling was difficult. The lighter Scottish pack matched the All Blacks in the loose and perhaps fortunately for Scotland, Don Clarke had a rare off-day with his boot. He missed five penalty attempts and neither side was able to take advantage of the other's mistakes. The final whistle went after a surge up field by Don Clarke came to nothing when his kick ahead was caught by his opposite number, Wilson, who calmly kicked the ball into touch. The whistle went and Scotland had denied the All Blacks their desired Grand Slam. On 12th November 1984 Scotland drew 25-25 with the All Blacks, but as every Kiwi will remind the Scots, they have never beaten them in over one hundred years of trying.

The All Blacks break from the scrum

The First Ever Player to Take 300 Test Wickets

In the annals of cricket history, the year 1963 stands out as a pinnacle for Fred Trueman, the fiery fast bowler from Yorkshire whose relentless pace wreaked havoc on opposing batsmen. Throughout the five Tests against the formidable West Indies, Trueman's ferocity saw a staggering 34 wickets tumble. However, as the cricketing world turned its attention to the arrival of Bobby Simpson's Australian squad in 1964, whispers began to circulate about Trueman's waning powers. Despite being only 33 years old, Trueman's once-dominant presence on the pitch seemed to be diminishing. The trademark stare, the menacing scowl, the unruly locks of hair whipping across his forehead, and the fiery intensity with which he hurled the ball remained unchanged, yet the frequency of wickets seemed to dwindle. Though he managed to add five scalps to his tally in the favourable conditions of Lords, the third Test at Headingley unfolded as a nightmare scenario for England's ageing pace spearhead. After England's dismissal for a modest 268, Trueman found himself tasked with breaking the Australian resistance.

Fred Trueman

However, in a frantic and farcical attempt to dislodge Peter Burge, Trueman resorted to a series of ill-executed deliveries, allowing Burge to dispatch them with ease. As Neil Hawke settled in to support Burge, England's hopes of a resurgence dwindled. The partnership flourished, aided by the obstinate resistance of Grout, propelling Australia to a formidable total of 389 and ultimately sealing England's fate. The aftermath of Headingley proved devastating for Trueman. Once hailed as England's go-to bowler, he found himself unceremoniously dropped from the squad, his career tally frozen at a tantalising 297 wickets. As the teams convened for the next encounter, a high-scoring 'bore-draw' at Headingley, Trueman's absence loomed large over the English camp. However, redemption beckoned at the Oval, albeit in the most unexpected of circumstances. While Trueman's bowling initially lacked its usual vigour, it was the spin wizardry of Fred Titmus that kept England in the game. Yet, on the third morning, just as hope began to wane, Trueman summoned his remaining reserves of skill and determination. With Australia cruising at 343 for 6, Ian Redpath and Tom Veivers threatened to put the game out of reach. But, in a moment of sheer brilliance, Trueman sent Redpath's middle-stump cartwheeling with a searing delivery. The following ball, a sharp outswinger, found the edge of McKenzie's bat, flying into the safe hands of Colin Cowdrey at slip. In an instant, Trueman found himself on the cusp of history, poised to become the first cricketer ever to claim 300 Test wickets. Trueman charged in with renewed determination, each delivery infused with an intensity that belied his years. Though denied a hat-trick by the resolute defense of Hawke, Trueman's moment of glory arrived soon after, as a fast delivery found the edge of Hawke's bat, nestling safely into the waiting hands of Cowdrey. The crowd erupted in jubilation, their thunderous applause echoing through the stadium as Trueman etched his name into the annals of cricketing immortality. For Fred Trueman, the journey from the wilderness of Headingley to the historic milestone at the Oval was a testament to his unwavering spirit and indomitable will. Trueman stood tall, a legend of the game, his legacy secure for generations to come.

Northern Dancer | The Little Horse with a Big Heart

He was known as "The little horse with a big heart", "Canada's Most Famous Racehorse" and "Sire of the Century"; and all for good reason. Northern Dancer was a champion whose descendants continue to dominate racing today. For what he lacked in stature he made up for in attitude. Born in 1961 on Windfield Farms in Oshawa, Ontario, Northern Dancer was "the little horse that could" and a constant underdog. As a yearling his owner, industrialist E.P. Taylor, put him up for auction with a reserve price of $25,000. Standing under 15 hands tall, there were no interested bidders so Taylor ended up taking Dancer home. The following year the two-year-old showed promise, making his debut at Fort Erie Racetrack in a 5½ furlong maiden race for Canadian-bred horses. Ridden by jockey Ron Turcotte

Northern Dancer

(who later went on to ride the Triple Crown Winner, Secretariat), the little horse pulled clear of seven other two-year-olds in the pack. The same year he would also win the Coronation Futurity and go on to be named the Canadian Champion Two-Year-Old Colt. His three-year-old campaign started with similar success, winning the Flamingo Stakes, Blue Grass Stakes

Northern Dancer's foal Nijinksy winning the Gladness Stakes in 1970

and Florida Derby before setting his sights on Kentucky in May of 1964. At the 90th running of the Kentucky Derby, Northern Dancer was the underdog battling the favourite, Hillside. In a tight race the Dancer won by a neck, becoming the first Canadian-bred colt to win the Derby while setting a track record of 2 minutes dead. Still the little Canadian horse "that could" wasn't done yet. He finished off his three-year-old campaign by winning the Queen's Plate at Woodbine Racetrack, Ontario. For his accomplishments in 1964 he was named both the US and Canadian Champion 3-year-old colt and Canadian Horse of the Year. Despite losing the Belmont and falling just one win shy of the Triple Crown, the mayor of Toronto declared 8th June 1964 to be "Northern Dancer Day". The idea of a ticker tape parade was cancelled due to the colt's highly strung personality. Amid all his success, Northern Dancer continued to race through July of 1964 until he bowed a tendon during a workout at Belmont that didn't respond to treatment. This effectively ended his racing career, so he was retired to stud. His first progeny reached racing age in 1968; Viceregal went undefeated and was named Horse of the Year in Canada. His second round of foals included Nijinsky, who went on to win the English Triple Crown of Guineas, Derby and St. Leger. His genes were so sought after in the early '70s that he was the leading sire in North America in 1971 as well as the leading sire in Great Britain and Ireland in 1970, '78, '83 and '84. According to the Jockey Club, Northern Dancer would sire 411 winners and 147 stakes winners from 645 registered foals; a win percentage of nearly 64%. 31 Epsom Derby winners, 37 Irish Derby winners and 26 Prix de l'Arc de Triomphe victors, have brave little Northern Dancer in their lineage.

John Surtees

John Norman Surtees, CBE (1934-2017) was a legendary British racing driver, widely considered one of the greatest drivers of all time. He is the only racing driver to have won world championships on both two wheels and four. Prior to his Formula One career he won seven world championships in the 1950s riding motorcycles. His trajectory into racing was encouraged by his father Jack Surtees, who was both a south London motorcycle dealer and grass track racer. John entered his first grass track race aged 15 in 1950. Just six years later he won the 500cc world championship riding an Italian MV Agusta bike. At the time he was given the nickname 'Figlio del vento' (son of the wind). Surtees would go on to double dominate motorcycle racing in the late 1950s winning both the 350cc and 500cc world champions in 1958, 1959 and 1960. He also won the Senior TT at the Isle of Man TT three years in a row. In 1960, he added two extra wheels to his racing vehicles making his Formula One debut for Team Lotus. During his first season, he made an impression with an impressive second place finish at the British Grand Prix. The following two seasons saw John

John Surtees (pictured in 1964)

race in a Cooper T53 and V8 Lola Mk4 respectively. However, for the 1963 season he would join Scuderia Ferrari. The following year, in 1964, three British drivers hotly contested the championship: Graham Hill in his BRM, Jim Clark in his Lotus-Climax and John Surtees in his Ferrari 158. The season went to a decider at the final round in Mexico. In a nail-biting finish, Clark was forced to stop on his last lap due to an oil leak. Hill was held up after a minor collision with Surtees' Ferrari teammate, Lorenzo Bandini. Bandini was then given team orders to give up his second place to Surtees. This gave Jim Surtees the driver's title by a single point. Ferrari would also win the manufacturer's cup. Although this was his only F1 season title, Surtees would continue racing until 1972. His career and life were nearly ended in an horrific crash in 1965 which left his body 4 inches shorter on one side to the other. He survived and continued to race. He would also go on to set up his own racing team, the Surtees Racing Organisation competing in F1 between 1970 and 1978.

Surtees (No.2) ahead in the 1964 Dutch Grand Prix

Surtees was a seven-time motorcycle world champion

The Day Cassius Clay Shook Up The World

25th February 1964 at the Convention Hall in Miami Beach

Cassius Clay

Cassius Clay, later Muhammed Ali, was the king of trash-talking before a fight. Some of it was witty, some of it was nasty, but it was all in the game. Before his World Championship fight with Sonny Liston he gave us both parts of his repertoire first saying: "If you like to lose your money, be a fool and bet on Sonny," followed by a more abusive: "After the fight, I'm gonna build myself a pretty home and use him as a bearskin rug. Liston even smells like a bear. I'm gonna give him to the local zoo after I whup him." A sizeable crowd of 8,300 spectators converged at the Convention Hall arena in Miami Beach, eagerly anticipating the showdown between Cassius Clay, affectionately dubbed the 'Louisville Lip', and the reigning champion, Liston. Clay, the perceived underdog, aimed to prove his mettle against the formidable Liston. The tide turned in Clay's favour early on as Liston, in a moment of misfortune, injured his shoulder in the opening round, hampering his ability to connect with his elusive opponent. By the seventh round, Clay astutely noticed Liston's discarded mouth guard, a subtle indication of the champion's distress. Seizing the moment, Clay flaunted his prowess in the ring, debuting his signature 'Ali Shuffle' to the delight of the crowd. Speculation swirled regarding Liston's injury, with some suggesting nefarious motives behind his apparent capitulation. Rumours of mafia involvement and a potential fixed outcome circulated, though concrete evidence remained elusive. Despite conjecture, Clay's triumph was undeniable, marking a historic moment in boxing history as he clinched the world heavyweight title.

In the aftermath of his victory, Clay celebrated at a Miami hotel alongside his confidant Malcolm X, a prominent figure within the African American Muslim community. Just days later, Clay's demeanour underwent a notable transformation as he publicly embraced the Nation of Islam, espousing its principles of racial segregation and embracing the virtues of his newfound faith. Clay adopted the name Muhammad Ali, symbolising his allegiance to his newfound beliefs. Ali's journey transcended the realms of sport, catapulting him into the pantheon of 20th century icons renowned as much for his social and political impact as for his athletic prowess.

The packed Miami Beach Convention Hall

However, Ali's principled stance against the Vietnam War would prove to be his most controversial yet defining moment. Refusing induction into the US Army on grounds of religious conviction, Ali faced backlash and condemnation leading to the stripping of his heavyweight title in 1967 and a subsequent legal battle. Despite facing adversity and a precipitous decline in popularity, particularly within the United States, Ali's steadfast commitment to his beliefs earned him admiration and respect worldwide. His legacy endures as a testament to courage, conviction, and the enduring power of principle over adversity.

The Open

Tony Lema's potential to carve his name into golfing history was tragically cut short, leaving a hole in the sport's pantheon of legends. His untimely demise at the age of 32 in Lansing robbed the golfing world of a talent that could have rivalled the likes of Jack Nicklaus and Arnold Palmer. Lema wasn't merely a rising star; he had already ascended to the pinnacle of his game, consistently outperforming the competition on the PGA tours of the 1950s and 60s. In 1964, Lema's dominance was unparalleled as he clinched victory in five PGA tournaments, securing his status as the year's preeminent golfer. His crowning achievement came at The Open, held at the home of golf St. Andrews, further cementing his reputation. His celebrity status was growing, propelling Lema into the spotlight with appearances on popular TV programmes like the Ed Sullivan Show. However, tragedy would strike after the 1966 PGA

Tony Lema with the 1964 Open trophy

Championship in Akron, Ohio, when Lema and his wife embarked on a fateful journey to the Lansing Hammond Airport en route to the Lincolnshire Country Club for an exhibition tournament. Fate intervened cruelly as their plane crashed just short of its destination on 24th June 1966. With a twist of horrible irony, the plane came down on the Lansing Country Golf Club claiming the lives of all four occupants, shattering the dreams and aspirations of a promising career. In remembrance of Lema, the 7th hole at the Lansing Country Club was dedicated to him with the erection of a memorial plaque.

The US Open

The US Open, played at the Congressional Country Club in the suburbs of Washington D.C. was a gruelling event played in near 100F heat. What compounded matters was that, up until 1964, the tournament was played over three days with the final two rounds being held on the final day. The leader entering the third round was Tommy Jacobs, who shot 64, tying the US Open record of that time for a second round score. Jacobs carded a third-round 70 and held a 2-stroke lead over Ken Venturi going into the final round. Venturi was showing signs of dehydration. He nearly collapsed on the 15th hole of the morning round, and walked and played slowly after that. But he continued, albeit followed by doctors. He tried to keep cool in the near 100F temperatures by using cold compresses and ice packs. As he staggered (sometimes literally) around the course that afternoon, Venturi kept making shots. He wound up shooting 70 to Jacobs' 76, claiming a four-stroke victory. When his final putt dropped into the cup, Venturi raised his arms and said, "My God, I've won the Open." Venturi's win was certainly a surprise. He hadn't won on the PGA Tour in four years, and hadn't even qualified for the US Open the previous three years. The next year, the rules were changed and the US Open was played over four days, as it is today.

The Ferrari 275 GTB was first produced in 1964. It's a two-seat grand touring coupé originally powered by a 3.3 litre V12 engine producing between 260 and 320 hp. Between 1964 and 1966, 442 examples of the Pininfarina-styled 275 GTB were produced. It often features in the Top 10 lists of the greatest Ferraris of all time.

The iconic Porsche 911 first went on sale in 1964. It replaced Porsche's smaller 356 model. The rear-engined, air-cooled 911 was originally going to be called the Porsche 901. However, Peugeot objected to using a name with three numbers with a zero in the middle in France as they claimed they had rights to this. The 901 became the 911 and the rest is history.

Another iconic car was launched in the second half of 1964. The Ford Mustang took the US by storm. Available as a hardtop, convertible and then a fastback, the Mustang started the 'pony class' of cars. These are compact and affordable coupés or convertibles with a performance edge. The car was immortalised in the 1968 film 'Bullitt'.

Manufactured in the Jensen factory in West Bromwich near Birmingham in the UK, the Sunbeam Tiger was a V8 high-performance version of the Sunbeam Alpine produced by the Rootes Group. AC Cobra designer Carroll Shelby worked on the Alpine's conversion. The car was produced between 1964 and 1967 when Chrysler took over the Rootes Group.

The first jar of Nutella left Ferrero's Italian factory on the 20th April 1964. The spread is based on 18th century gianduja, chocolate blended with 30% hazelnut paste. Pietro Ferrero, a baker from Alba, used to sell gianduja in solid blocks. In 1951, he created a creamy version called Supercrema Gianduja. From this, his son Michele created the Nutella empire.

On the 28th December 1964, Diet Pepsi was launched to the US market. Originally called Patio Diet Cola in test markets it was sold in both glass bottles and cans. It competed with the Coca-Cola's Company's Tab sugar free drink which was launched a year earlier. It would be nearly 20 years later when it was launched in the UK in 1983 as Pepsi Diet.

The now ubiquitous Sharpie marker first went on sale in the US in 1964. It was created and manufactured by the Sanford Ink Company whose history dates back to 1857. The Sharpie was the first pen-style permanent marker. Due to their ease of use, even in zero gravity, they became the pen of choice for astronauts on-board the international space station.

The 8-track tape format was launched in 1964. It became popular in the US, Canada and the UK, especially for use in cars. Unlike compact cassette, the 8-track tape was an endless loop so the cartridge did not need to be ejected. Once the 80 minutes of audio had played, it was would start at the beginning again. It was popular until the early 1980s.

Photo Credits

Credits shown in the order in which they appear in the book. Photos not listed are in the public domain.

Key to page numbers

fc = front cover; **ifc** = inside front cover; **tp** = title page; **cp** = contents page; **ap1** = acknowledgements page 1; **ap2** = acknowledgements page 2; **ibc** = inside back cover; **bc** = back cover; **3** = page 3; **4** = page 4; etc.

Key to object position on page

tl = top left; *t* = top; *tc* = top centre; *tr* = top right; *cla* = centre left above; *ca* = centre above; *cra* = centre right above; *cl* = centre left; *c* = centre; *cr* = centre right; *clb* = centre left below; *cb* = centre below; *crb* = centre right below; *bl* = bottom left; *b* = bottom; *bc* = bottom centre; *br* = bottom right; *w* = whole page; *h* = header; *tb* = text background

Key to image licence types

CC BY-SA 2.0 = https://creativecommons.org/licenses/by-sa/2.0/deed.en;
CC BY-SA 3.0 = https://creativecommons.org/licenses/by-sa/3.0/deed.en;
CC BY-SA 4.0 = https://creativecommons.org/licenses/by-sa/4.0/deed.en;
(m) = image has been modified as permitted under licensing terms

fc *ca*: Paul McCartney & John Lennon (m) © Eric Koch for Anefo, Wikimedia Commons, CC BY-SA 3.0; **fc** *cra*: Peter Sellers (m) © 7th Street Theatre Hoquiam, Flickr.com, CC BY-SA 2.0; **tp** *w*: Porsche 911 (m) © GUIDO - stock.adobe.com; **3** *tr*: Arthur Ashe © Art Rogers, Los Angeles Times, Wikimedia Commons, CC BY-SA 4.0; **4** *clb*: The Beatles © VARA, Wikimedia Commons, CC BY-SA 3.0; **5** *cla*: Bluebird © Motoring Picture Library / Alamy Stock Photo; **17** *cla*: Jane Horrocks © Matt Crossick / Alamy Stock Photo; **17** *clb*: Elle Macpherson © Eva Rinaldi, Wikimedia Commons, CC BY-SA 2.0; **18** *cla*: Tracy Chapman © Hans Hillewaert, Wikimedia Commons, CC BY-SA 4.0; **18** *clb*: Andy Serkis © Super Festivals, Wikimedia Commons, CC BY-SA 2.0; **19** *cla*: David Baddiel © Brian Minkoff-London Pixels, Wikimedia Commons, CC BY-SA 3.0; **19** *clb*: Kathy Burke © PA Images / Alamy Stock Photo; **20** *cla*: Boris Johnson © Ben Shread, Wikimedia Commons, CC BY-SA 3.0; **20** *clb*: Sandra Bullock © Eva Rinaldi, Wikimedia Commons, CC BY-SA 2.0; **21** *cla*: Jürgen Klinsmann © Steffen Prößdorf, Wikimedia Commons, CC BY-SA 4.0; **21** *clb*: Keanu Reeves © Governo do Estado de São Paulo, Wikimedia Commons, CC BY-SA 2.0; **22** *cla*: Susie Dent © United Agents / www.unitedagents.co.uk; **21** *clb*: Harry Hill © Moviemaker33, Wikimedia Commons, CC BY-SA 4.0; **22** *cla*: Clive Owen © Mario Antonio Pena Zapateria, Wikimedia Commons, CC BY-SA 2.0; **23** *clb row 1*: Nicholas Cage © Gerald Geronimo, Wikimedia Commons, CC BY-SA 2.0; **23** *cb row 1*: Christopher Eccleston © Super Festivals, Wikimedia Commons, CC BY-SA 2.0; **23** *crb row 1*: Matt Dillon © David Shankbone, Wikimedia Commons, CC BY-SA 3.0; **23** *clb row 2*: Prince Edward © UKinUSA, Wikimedia Commons, CC BY-SA 2.0; **23** *cb row 2*: Neneh Cherry © Frankie Fouganthin, Wikimedia Commons, CC BY-SA 3.0; **23** *crb row 2*: Rob Lowe © David Shankbone, Wikimedia Commons, CC BY-SA 3.0; **23** *clb row 3*: Lenny Kravitz © Gage Skidmore, Wikimedia Commons, CC BY-SA 3.0; **23** *cb row 3*: Courteney Cox © Felicia C. Sullivan, Wikimedia Commons, CC BY-SA 3.0; **23** *crb row 3*: David Morrissey © Gage Skidmore, Wikimedia Commons, CC BY-SA 2.0; **23** *clb row 4*: Ross Kemp © Damien Everett, Wikimedia Commons, CC BY-SA 2.0; **23** *cb row 4*: Bonnie Langford © AnemoneProjectors, Wikimedia Commons, CC BY-SA 4.0; **23** *crb row 4*: Sarah Lancashire © dalekhelen, Wikimedia Commons, CC BY-SA 2.0; **23** *clb row 5*: Greg Wallace © Richard Gillin, Wikimedia Commons, CC BY-SA 2.0; **23** *crb row 5*: Famke Janssen © Gage Skidmore, Wikimedia Commons, CC BY-SA 3.0; **25** *tl*: Ian Fleming © Bradford Timeline, Flickr.com, CC BY-SA 2.0; **27** *tl*: Coins © Jo Smiley Hailey, Unsplash.com; **27** *tr*: House © Sludgegulper, Wikimedia Commons, CC BY-SA 2.0; **27** *cla*: Ford Cortina © Charles01, Wikimedia Commons, CC BY-SA 3.0; **27** *bl*: Olympia Typewriter © Rainer P. A. Wermke, Wikimedia Commons, CC BY-SA 4.0; **27** *bc*: Milk Bottles © Jason Murphy, Unsplash.com; **27** *br*: Petrol pump © Erik Mclean, Unsplash.com; **28** *tr*: Rubber Plantation © with thanks to John Lewis; **30** *tc*: Chickens © Mohammad Someea, Wikimedia Commons, CC BY-SA 4.0; **30** *tr*: Whisky Barrels © Bbadgett, Wikimedia Commons, CC BY-SA 3.0; **36** *cra*: Gratin Dauphinois © Ludovic Péron, Wikimedia Commons, CC BY-SA 3.0; **37** *c*: Spotted Dick © Tracy, Wikimedia Commons, CC BY-SA 2.0; **38** *tr*: SS Canberra © John Ward, Wikimedia Commons, CC BY-SA 3.0; **39** *all photos* © with thanks to Jenny Freebairn; **42** *tr*: Broadcasting House © Redvers, Wikimedia Commons, CC BY-SA 3.0; **43** *clb*: Goldfinger © ETH-Bibliothek Zürich, Bildarchiv / Fotograf: Comet Photo AG (Zürich) / Com_C13-035-005, Wikimedia Commons, CC BY-SA 4.0; **44** *cla*: A Hard Day's Night © Luckhardt, Wikimedia Commons, CC BY-SA 3.0; **44** *cra*: Peter Sellers © Pictorial Press Ltd / Alamy Stock Photo; **46** *clb*: Noele Gordon © with thanks to The Noele Gordon Archive, www.noelegordon.co.uk; **47** *clb*: Playschool Toys © Chemical Engineer, Wikimedia Commons, CC BY-SA 4.0; **48** *cla*: Seven Up! © Everett Collection Inc / Alamy Stock Photo; **48** *clb*: Top of the Pops background image © Chris Walter, Wikimedia Commons, CC BY-SA 3.0; **49** *cla*: Entertaining Mr. Sloane (m) © Robyn Bartlett, Flickr.com, CC BY-SA 2.0; **50** *tl* & **53** *tr*: The Animals © Richard William Laws, Wikimedia Commons, CC BY-SA 3.0; **50** *cl* & **53** *bl* & **53** *crb*: Roy Orbison © Jack de Nijs for Anefo, Wikimedia Commons, CC BY-SA 4.0; **52** *bl*: Lulu © R. Frings, Wikimedia Commons, CC BY-SA 3.0; **52** *cl*: Petula Clark © ETH-Bibliothek Zürich, Bildarchiv / Fotograf: Baumann, Heinz / Com_L15-0036-0002-0004, Wikimedia Commons, CC BY-SA 4.0; **53** *clb*: Sandie Shaw © Ron Kroon, Nationaal Archief, Den Haag, Rijksfotoarchief: Fotocollectie Algemeen Nederlands Fotopersbureau (ANEFO), Wikimedia Commons, CC BY-SA 3.0; **55** *clb*: Morecambe and Wise © Pictorial Press Ltd / Alamy Stock Photo; **56** *tr*: Andy Warhol © Jack Mitchell, Wikimedia Commons, CC BY-SA 4.0; **56** *br*: Ian Fleming © Bradford Timeline, Flickr.com, CC BY-SA 2.0; **57-59** All images created with the assistance of DALL·E 3/ Adobe Photoshop; **60** *bl*: Single Form © AndyScott, Wikimedia Commons, CC BY-SA 4.0; **61** *tl*: John Masefield © Los Angeles Times, Wikimedia Commons, CC BY-SA 2.0; **61** *br*: Carol Ann Duffy © walnut whippet, Wikimedia Commons, CC BY-SA 2.0; **63** *cla*: ESRO Control Room © ESA, Wikimedia Commons, CC BY-SA 3.0; **63** *bl*: Voskhod 1 © Andrew Gray, Wikimedia Commons, CC BY-SA 3.0; **64** *t*: Unisphere © Anthony Conti, Wikimedia Commons, CC BY-SA 2.0; **65** *clb*: Chrysler Pavilion © wilford peloquin, Wikimedia Commons, CC BY-SA 2.0; **65** *cb*: Johnson Wax Pavilion © Doug Coldwell, Wikimedia Commons, CC BY-SA 3.0; **65** *crb*: Lincoln animatronic © Harshlight, Wikimedia Commons, CC BY-SA 2.0; **67** *tl*: MiG-25 © Leonid Faerberg (transport-photo.com), Wikimedia Commons, GNU Free v1.2; **68** *tr*: Donald Campbell © Auge=mit, Wikimedia Commons, CC BY-SA 4.0; **68** *cl*: Bluebird K7 © Sheppane at English Wikipedia, Wikimedia Commons, CC BY-SA 3.0; **68** *br*: Bluebird CN7 © Motoring Picture Library / Alamy Stock Photo; **71** *tr*: Youths escaping with injured © Peruvian Institute of Sport; **71** *bl*: Estadio Nacional © Chalisimo5 , Wikimedia Commons, CC BY-SA 3.0; **74** *t*: Bristol Brittannia © Ken Fielding, Wikimedia Commons, CC BY-SA 3.0; **76** *tr*: Mary Rand © Eric Koch for Anefo, Wikimedia Commons, CC BY-SA 3.0; **81** *tr*: Fred Trueman © PA Images / Alamy Stock Photo;

continued on next page...

Photo Credits continued

82 *clb*: Nijinsky © Sirlad, Wikimedia Commons, CC BY-SA 4.0; **83** *bl*: Surtees and Gurney © Harry Pot , Wikimedia Commons, CC BY-SA 3.0; **84** *tl*: Cassius Clay © Dutch National Archives, Wikimedia Commons, CC BY-SA 3.0; **85** *tr*: Tony Lema © PA Images / Alamy Stock Photo; **86** *t*: Ferrari 275 (m) © Mr.choppers, Wikimedia Commons, CC BY-SA 3.0; **86** *b*: Porsche 911 (m) © Alexander Migl, Wikimedia Commons, CC BY-SA 4.0; **87** *t*: Ford Mustang (m) © GerdeeX, Wikimedia Commons, CC BY-SA 4.0; **87** *b*: Sunbeam Tiger (m) © Steve Brown, Wikimedia Commons, CC BY-SA 2.0; **88** *t*: Nutella (m) © Janine, Flickr.com, CC BY-SA 2.0; **88** *b*: Diet Pepsi (m) © Steve Cukrov / Alamy Stock Photo; **89** *t*: Sharpie Pens (m) © RRRST, Wikimedia Commons, CC BY-SA 4.0; **89** *b*: 8-track (m) © Leonard Nevarez, Wikimedia Commons, CC BY-SA 2.0; **92** *tc*: Coffee Table (m) © Sincerely Media, Unsplash.com; **BC** *tl*: The Rolling Stones (m) © Hugo van Gelderen (ANEFO), Wikimedia Commons, CC BY-SA 3.0; **BC** *cla*: Surtees and Gurney (m) © Harry Pot / Anefo, Wikimedia Commons, CC BY-SA 3.0; **BC** *tr*: Millie Small (m) © Harry Pot / Anefo, Wikimedia Commons, CC BY-SA 3.0;

Graphic and Background Image Credits

Credits shown in the order in which they appear in the book.

Additional Key

(ic) = icon; (ph) = photo

fc *c*, **tp** *ca* & **bc**: (ph) Texture (m) © Felipe Santana, unsplash.com; **2-15**: (ph) Wood (m) © Michael Schwarzenberger, pixabay.com; **2-3, 16-91** *tb*: (ph) Paper Texture (m) © rawpixel.com; **3** *cla*: (ic) Play (m) © Adrien Coquet, thenounproject.com, CC BY-SA 3.0; **6,8,10,12,14** *tl* & **7,9,11,13,15** *tr*: (ic) Newspaper (m) © Loic Poivet, thenounproject.com, CC BY-SA 3.0; **6-15** *c*: (ph) Book (m) © Robert Armstrong, pixabay.com; **16,18,20,22** *tl* & **17,19,21,23** *tr*: (ic) Birthday Calendar (m) © Kiran Shastry, thenounproject.com, CC BY-SA 3.0; **16-25, 42-61, 86-92** *w*: (m)(ph) Concrete Terrazzo Wall (m) © rawpixel.com;

16 *cla*: (ic) Computer (m) © Damong, thenounproject.com, CC BY-SA 3.0; **16** *clb* & **20** *cla* & **24** *cl* & **24** *clb*: (ic) Speaker (m) © popcornarts, thenounproject.com, CC BY-SA 3.0; **17,23,24** *cla* (ic) Theatre (m) © Ben Davis, thenounproject.com, CC BY-SA 3.0; **17** *clb* (ic) Mannequin (m) © Blair Adams, thenounproject.com, CC BY-SA 3.0; **22** *cla*: (ic) Microphone (m) © andriwidodo, thenounproject.com, CC BY-SA 3.0; **18,20,21** *tr*: (ic) Clapper Board (m) © Andrew Nielsen, thenounproject.com, CC BY-SA 3.0; **19** *cla* & **19,22** *clb*: (ic) Theatre Comedy (m) © b farias, thenounproject.com, CC BY-SA 3.0; **21** *cla*: (ic) Football (m) © leo-graph.com, thenounproject.com, CC BY-SA 3.0; **22** *cla*: (ic) Television (m) © Adrien Coquet, thenounproject.com, CC BY-SA 3.0; **23** *clb*: (ic) Baby (m) © Emily Keller, thenounproject.com, CC BY-SA 3.0; **24** *tl* & **25** *tr*: (ic) Wreath (m) © Alex Muravev, thenounproject.com, CC BY-SA 3.0; **25** *cla* & **25** *clb*: (ic) Book (m) © Travis Avery, thenounproject.com, CC BY-SA 3.0; **25** *cl*: (ic) Music Note (m) © karen tyler, thenounproject.com, CC BY-SA 3.0; **26-40** *w*: (m)(ph) White Concrete Wall (m) © rawpixel.com; **26** *tl* & **27** *tr*: (ic) Coins (m) © Evgenii Likhachov, thenounproject.com, CC BY-SA 3.0; **28** *tl*: (ic) Earth (m) © David Khai, thenounproject.com, CC BY-SA 3.0; **29** *tr*: (ic) Office (m) © Anggara Putra, thenounproject.com, CC BY-SA 3.0; **30** *tl*: (ic) Tractor (m) © Olivier Guin, thenounproject.com, CC BY-SA 3.0; **31** *tr*: (ic) School Desk (m) © Jongrak, thenounproject.com, CC BY-SA 3.0; **32** *tl*: (ic) Exams (m) © Arjan Farzkenari, thenounproject.com, CC BY-SA 3.0; **33** *tr*: (ic) Children (m) © IronSV, thenounproject.com, CC BY-SA 3.0; **34** *tl* & **35** *tr*: (ic) Home (m) © Numero Uno, thenounproject.com, CC BY-SA 3.0; **36** *tl*: (ic) Potato (m) © Firza Alamsyah (m) © faisalovers, thenounproject.com, CC BY-SA 3.0; **37** *tr*: (ic) Pudding (m) © Ranah Pixel, thenounproject.com, CC BY-SA 3.0; **38** *tl* & **39** *tr*: (ic) Holiday (m) © Claudia Revalina, thenounproject.com, CC BY-SA 3.0; **40** *tl*: (ic) Fashion (m) © Mahmure Alp, thenounproject.com, CC BY-SA 3.0; **41** *tr*: (ic) Christmas Tree (m) © Azam Ishaq, thenounproject.com, CC BY-SA 3.0; **41** *w*: (ic) Christmas (m) © Annie Spratt, unsplash.com; **42** *tl*: (ic) Radio (m) © GreenHill, thenounproject.com, CC BY-SA 3.0; **43,45** *tr* & **44** *tl*: (ic) Clapper Board (m) © Andrew Nielsen, thenounproject.com, CC BY-SA 3.0; **46,48** *tl* & **47** *tr*: (ic) Television (m) © Adrien Coquet, thenounproject.com, CC BY-SA 3.0; **49** *cra* (ic) Theatre (m) © Ben Davis, thenounproject.com, CC BY-SA 3.0; **50,52** *tl* & **51** *tr*: (ic) Record (m) © Mourad Mokrane, thenounproject.com, CC BY-SA 3.0; **53** *tr*: (ic) Music Note (m) © karen tyler, thenounproject.com, CC BY-SA 3.0; **54** *tl* & **55** *tr*: (ic) Trumpet (m) © Valter Bispo, thenounproject.com, CC BY-SA 3.0; **56** *tl*: (ic) Arts (m) © Kelsey Armstrong, thenounproject.com, CC BY-SA 3.0; **57,59** *tr* & **58** *tl*: (ic) Book (m) © Travis Avery, thenounproject.com, CC BY-SA 3.0; **60** *tl*: (ic) Sculpture (m) © Creative Mania, thenounproject.com, CC BY-SA 3.0; **61** *tr*: (ic) Poetry (m) © Martin, thenounproject.com, CC BY-SA 3.0; **62-67** *w*: (ph) Plasma (m) © Hal Gatewood, unsplash.com; **62** *tl* & **63** *tr*: (ic) Space (m) © Trevor Dsouza, thenounproject.com, CC BY-SA 3.0; **64** *tl* & **65** *tr*: (ic) Fair (m) © Amethyst Studio, thenounproject.com, CC BY-SA 3.0; **66** *tl* & **67** *tr*: (ic) Fighter Jet (m) © Nico Ilk, thenounproject.com, CC BY-SA 3.0; **68** *tl*: (ic) Speed (m) © indra anis, thenounproject.com, CC BY-SA 3.0; **68** *w*: (ph) Salt Flats (m) © Dietmar Rabich, Wikimedia Commons, CC BY-SA 4.0; **69** *tr*: (ic) Train (m) © Sierra Pennalar, thenounproject.com, CC BY-SA 3.0; **69** *w*: (ph) Train Line (m) © Ben Garratt, unsplash.com; **70** *tl*: (ic) Earthquake (m) © KonKapp, thenounproject.com, CC BY-SA 3.0; **70** *w*: (ph) Earthquake Damage (m) © Jose Antonio Gallego Vázquez, unsplash.com; **71** *tr*: (ic) Tear Gas (m) © Dio Sugiharto, thenounproject.com, CC BY-SA 3.0; **71** *w*: (ph) Football Stadium (m) © Emerson Vieira, unsplash.com; **72** *tl*: (ic) USA flag (m) © Joel Wisneski, thenounproject.com, CC BY-SA 3.0; **72** *w*: (ph) Dealey Plaza © Renelibrary, Wikimedia Commons, CC BY-SA 4.0; **73** *tr*: (ic) Gavel (m) © DinosoftLabs, thenounproject.com, CC BY-SA 3.0; **73** *w*: (ph) Courtroom (m) © Museums of History New South Wales, unsplash.com; **74** *tl*: (ic) boeing b 29 superfortress (m) © usubaliev, thenounproject.com, CC BY-SA 3.0; **74** *w*: (ph) Lancaster Bomber (m) © Paul, adobestock.com; **75** *tr*: (ic) nobel peace prize (m) © Tom Fricker, thenounproject.com, CC BY-SA 3.0; **75** *w*: (ph) Auditorium (m) © Wan San Yip, unsplash.com; **76** *tl* & **77** *tr*: (ic) Olympic Rings (m) © sachan, thenounproject.com, CC BY-SA 3.0; **76** *w*: (ph) Athletics (m) © Braden Collum, unsplash.com; **76** *h*: (ph) Closing Ceremony © Project Kei, Wikimedia Commons, CC BY-SA 4.0; **77** *w*: (ph) Stadium (m) © Helsinki City Museum, Wikimedia Commons, CC BY-SA 4.0; **78** *tl*: (ic) Football (m) © leo-graph.com, thenounproject.com, CC BY-SA 3.0; **78** *w*: (ph) Football Pitch (m) © Alberto Frías, unsplash.com; **79** *tr*: (ic) Tennis (m) © Mister Pixel, thenounproject.com, CC BY-SA 3.0; **79** *w*: (ph) Tennis Court (m) © Max Zindel, unsplash.com; **80** *tl*: (ic) Rugby Ball (m) © Marco Livolsi, thenounproject.com, CC BY-SA 3.0; **80** *w*: (ph) Rugby Match (m) © Alex Motoc, unsplash.com; **80** *h*: (ph) Rugby Lineout © Auckland Museum, Wikimedia Commons, CC BY-SA 4.0; **81** *tr*: (ic) Cricket (m) © Bernd Lakenbrink, thenounproject.com, CC BY-SA 3.0; **81** *w*: (ph) Cricketer (m) © Yogendra Singh, unsplash.com; **82** *tl*: (ic) Horse Racing (m) © Sergio Morozov, thenounproject.com, CC BY-SA 3.0; **82** *w*: (ph) Racehorse (m) © Luisa Peter, unsplash.com; **82** *h*: (ph) Horse Race © Jongsun Lee, Wikimedia Commons, CC BY-SA 3.0; **83** *tr*: (ic) Race Car (m) © Slidicon, thenounproject.com, CC BY-SA 3.0; **83** *w*: (ph) Chequered Flag (m) © Bas van den Eijkhof, unsplash.com; **83** *h*: (ph) Old Race Car (m) © Jeff Cooper, unsplash.com; **84** *tl*: (ic) Boxing Glove (m) © Anton Anuchin, thenounproject.com, CC BY-SA 3.0; **84** *w*: (ph) Boxing Match (m) © Johann Walter Bantz, unsplash.com; **85** *tr*: (ic) Golfer (m) © Nicolas Vicent, thenounproject.com, CC BY-SA 3.0; **85** *w*: (ph) Golfing (m) © Courtney Cook, unsplash.com; **85** *h*: (ph) Golf Ball (m) © mk. s, unsplash.com; **86,88** *tl* & **87,89** *tr*: (ic) Framed Picture (m) © Lil Squid, thenounproject.com, CC BY-SA 3.0; **90** *tl* & **91** *tr*: (ic) Camera (m) © AomAm, thenounproject.com, CC BY-SA 3.0; **92** *tl*: (ic) Present (m) © Vinzence Studio, thenounproject.com, CC BY-SA 3.0

1964 : What A Year To Be Born!
Why not join our mailing list...

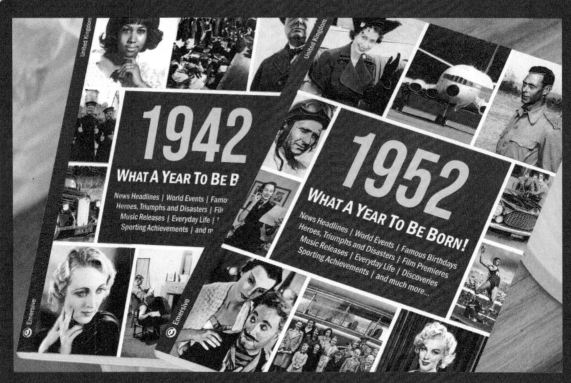
Answers to the Eleven-plus Exam on page 32

Arithmetic Questions

Q1: London to Birmingham is 120 miles
Q2: Christmas Day will fall on a Thursday
Q3: It will take 6 hours and 40 minutes
Q4: Five hundred and twenty three
Q5: A) John's mother was 40 years old
Q5: B) In 3 years' time
Q5: C) John will be 30 years old

General English Questions

Q1: A) Our dogs are carrying sticks.
Q1: B) Their butchers have no meat.
Q1: C) Men who like football are sure to have team scarves in their houses.
Q2: A) Finger
Q2: B) Umpire
Q2: C) Spaniards
Q3: A) Certain or sure
Q3: B) Shortly or soon
Q3: C) Decided

Printed in Great Britain
by Amazon

55061437R00053